PRAISE FOR MOLLY FLETCHER
AND *A WINNER'S GUIDE TO NEGOTIATING*

Molly Fletcher is a trailblazer within the sports industry. As one of the first female sports agents, she built a client base that includes some of the biggest names in sports both on and off the field. Molly has had a positive influence on her clients and on the many who look up to her.

Molly has been a hit as a speaker at many PGA TOUR Executive Women's Days, sharing her powerful message with executives at PGA TOUR events around the country. *A Winner's Guide to Negotiating: How Conversation Gets Deals Done* shares her unique perspective and insight gleaned from years of successful negotiating. This book is a useful tool to help you prepare for this important skill.

—Tim Finchem, commissioner of the PGA TOUR

Many assume strong negotiations are only conducted adversarially, nose-to-nose. Molly Fletcher demonstrates how a shoulder-to-shoulder approach, rooted in trust, giving, communication, and relationships drives ideal outcomes while building sustainable benefit and positive reputations. This book is a must-read and a must-follow for anyone who wants to be more effective.

—Kat Cole, president of Cinnabon, Inc.
and cofounder of Changers of Commerce

For Molly, negotiating breakout wins is muscle memory from honed fundamentals. This book provides useful tools to those who want to learn how to get dramatic deals done. A must-read.

—Sarah Palisi Chapin, partner and CEO of
Hail Merry Snack Foods

In *A Winner's Guide to Negotiating*, Molly Fletcher proves that successful negotiation is *not* an accident. Fresh, highly relevant, and easy to read, this book will be a game-changer for anyone who negotiates anything. A must-read for you and everyone on your team!

—Tommy Newberry, *New York Times* bestselling author of
The 4:8 Principle and *Success Is Not an Accident*

Powerful lessons told in an incredibly engaging way through stories we can all relate to. I didn't want to stop reading. I wanted to absorb every single lesson!

—Debbie Storey, senior vice president of talent development
and chief diversity officer at AT&T

A WINNER'S GUIDE

to
Negotiating

How Conversation
Gets Deals Done

Molly Fletcher

New York   Chicago   San Francisco   Athens   London
Madrid   Mexico City   Milan   New Delhi
Singapore   Sydney   Toronto

1 2 3 4 5 6 7 8 9 0   QFR/QFR   1 2 0 9 8 7 6 5 4

ISBN   978-0-07-183878-8
MHID   0-07-183878-3

e-ISBN 978-0-07-183880-1
e-MHID   0-07-183880-5

Library of Congress Cataloging-in-Publication Data

Fletcher, Molly
  A winner's guide to negotiating : how conversation gets deals done / by Molly Fletcher.
      pages cm
  Includes bibliographical references and index.
  ISBN 978-0-07-183878-8 (alk. paper)—ISBN 0-07-183878-3 (alk. paper)
1. Negotiation in business. 2. Negotiation. I. Title.
  HD58.6.F593 2015
  158'.5—dc23   2014017245

McGraw-Hill Education books are available at special quantity discounts to use as premiums and sales promotions or for use in corporate training programs. To contact a representative, please visit the Contact Us pages at www.mhprofessional.com

To Fred, Emma, Meg, Kate,
Mom, Dad, Jim, and John

Contents

Foreword

Great negotiators understand the power of stories. Stories connect us, and connection is at the heart of successful negotiations. The more you know people's stories, the more you see what they want and fear, what they will give up, and what they need to protect. Stories cut through the noise of daily life and constant information to provide understanding and meaning. The very best storytellers have always been the people with the greatest reach and influence.

In our dramatically changing digital world of multiple platforms and technology, storytelling is morphing. The speed and urgency of business is increasing. Now more than ever, a negotiator's success depends on integrity. There is so much information and data available to everyone today that it is even more critical to be a trusted source. Negotiating well depends on trust.

In this book, a great negotiator and a great storyteller has mined her deep experience in one of the most pressurized arenas of American business—negotiating professional sports contracts. Molly Fletcher understands the narrative of a successful deal and moves fluidly between five transparent, powerful steps. These steps are her code that helps her see the next possible move in a negotiation, prepare well, and maximize the results. Her personal anecdotes—often fascinating situations from her real-life experiences involving well-known sports figures—make these lessons easy to learn. This book is a prime example of storytelling to demystify a skill that is critical for success in business and relationships. It uses the case method to teach its lessons.

Great negotiators aspire to Molly's reputation for impeccable reliability, influence, and leadership. This is far from easy among wary clients like those in pro sports. Often, their careers are relatively brief. A lot of money is at stake. She faced another challenge: her clients were used to seeing men in her role. Creating the emotional attachments necessary for success takes a lot of guts; double that for a groundbreaking pioneer like Molly.

Reading her stories, I am reminded of her equal measure of grace. Because she knows that the heart of negotiations is strong relationships, she can salvage the opportunity to try again even when a deal falls apart. Few people can maintain relationships as authentically as Molly, and this book is her clear road map for readers to get to that pinnacle. As you read the book, you also realize that in order to be a great storyteller and great negotiator, you have to start by being a great listener. Understand your subjects by listening to them, and understand your counterparts on the other side of the table by truly hearing what they are trying to accomplish in your negotiation.

Today, so many voices vie for our attention on any subject, from the mundane to the most important. Molly's is one worth listening to about a skill that we all could be better at. With regard to negotiation and relationships, she nails it. By reading this book and applying its lessons, you can, too.

LARRY KRAMER
President and publisher of *USA Today*
Founder of MarketWatch
Author of *C-Scape: Conquer the Forces Changing Business Today*

Acknowledgments

This book is the result of a team effort.

My gratitude goes out to my amazing, wonderful, and awesome husband, Fred. His humble brilliance and support of our daughters and me are magical. He is an all-star father to our three daughters, Emma, Meg, and Kate. His professional success in commercial real estate and personal passion for solving fifth-grade math problems for our girls don't go unnoticed. He is the coach for everything, a leader—and even Santa Claus. Really close to perfect. I learn from him and am grateful for his strong faith and consistent love. Thank you to my girls, who are at the heart of my every decision and who keep me centered. They are each magically unique, despite all three being just 12 months apart in age (singleton and then twins). They are like sponges, and I wake up every day hoping to fill their sponges so they can enter the world and be their best selves.

Thank you to my parents and my brothers, who laid the foundation for much of my formative experiences around deal making and the philosophies that I now share with numerous corporate audiences and clients around the country. Whether negotiating my way out of getting beaten up by my big brothers or listening to my parents' stories from work, I learned every day that deals are everywhere—and so are the tools to make them work for me. Some of the most important negotiations involved ensuring that my brother didn't lick all my mom's amazing chocolate chip cookies when they came out of the oven.

Thank you to my team, especially Sprague Paynter, whose brilliance and support helped build the framework for this book, and Tiffany Allen, who scoured our sources, stories, and stats for the book. Without your support, this book wouldn't be here today.

Thank you to Michelle Hiskey, a brilliant writer who I am truly honored to have supporting me in the writing of this book. She knows sports, she knows me, she knows deals, and she is smart as heck. I am humbled to have her as a partner on this project.

Thank you to my agent, John Willig, a man of high integrity with healthy and transparent relationships. Thank you to my editor, Casey Ebro, for her guidance and support. It's an honor to be a member of her team at McGraw-Hill. They made the process fun and efficient.

Introduction

I crouched in the closet in my daughter's bedroom on Easter weekend 2007. It's not exactly where most sports agents do their deals, but that is where I found myself trying to negotiate to keep a big client, Michigan State head basketball coach Tom Izzo.

Tom and I are good friends today, but in that moment you would not have known it. News travels like lightning in the small universe of college basketball's elite coaches, and his future and our relationship were on the line.

What unfolded that week of the NCAA Final Four, the pinnacle of Tom's sport, was a chess match. Anything can happen in high-stakes negotiation, and no matter what you're negotiating, no doubt the stakes are high to you.

Izzo is a brilliant college basketball coach, an eight-time national coach of the year, a guy who sends players to the NBA all the time, and someone who—like most at his level—doesn't want to be taken for granted. As a seasoned sports agent, neither did I. However, I knew there were a few agents who could take my place but there was only one Tom Izzo.

In the middle of the Final Four, Kentucky expressed interest in Tom. If you know anything about college basketball, you know this is one of the most high-profile positions in all of coaching, one that almost every college coach would entertain. But like most negotiations, this one was a delicate dance between Tom's passion for Michigan State and what the folks in the Bluegrass State were looking for in their next head coach.

Some coaches are so hungry for a certain position or university that they will literally beg for the job, but Izzo had told us that under no circumstances would he do that. "We'll interview them as much as they interview you," we agreed.

Kentucky, though, had many choices. First, they offered the job to Billy Donovan, another client of ours, who quickly said no the day after the Final Four. Next, they turned to Rick Barnes, the coach at Texas. When Barnes turned them down, their egos were bruised, and so they moved to a hurry-up offense. They wanted desperately for someone to say yes, someone who would crawl to Lexington to coach.

Athletic directors certainly don't call agents to let them know their next move, and so we try to find out their moves through inside sources as quickly as possible. But the move from Donovan to Barnes surprised us. We thought their next ask would certainly be Tom.

Only it wasn't. The call went to Billy Gillispie. Not Tom Izzo. In my opinion, this was because they knew Gillispie would take it for sure.

I was in bed asleep at 2 a.m. when Izzo called. I had barely answered when Tom launched into me. I had seen him countless times on the sidelines of the court, down to the last seconds of close games, and knew he had this kind of temper, but it had never been unleashed on me. After all, I was the person he counted on to help him and the reason he hired our firm five years earlier. He knew we delivered.

After an hour of unloading his frustration on me, he hung up. All I had was a dazed "oh my" feeling. What just happened? Trust is everything in my business, and it wasn't just Izzo I might be losing.

But my oldest daughter, then age five, needed me. When she woke up, I hustled to her room to rub her back so that she could go back to sleep. In five minutes, she was sound asleep, but when she awakened again at 6 a.m., I was still staring at the ceiling.

Word of mouth is everything, and the trust I had carefully nurtured with Izzo was the foundation of our relationship and my ability to reach out to more elite coaches and represent them. Was it all crashing down now?

I knew I needed Izzo, but I didn't need anyone to speak to me like that. There were serious consequences for tolerating it. Backing down to him could make me a doormat, which would also doom my negotiating position. We and Tom knew that Kentucky's first ask had been Billy Donovan, and so I paced for two days trying to figure out my next move. Sleepless. Before I could negotiate *for* Izzo, I had to negotiate *with* Izzo and with myself.

As an agent, I work in a tight gap between where elite performers like Izzo shine and where they want to—or could—go next. There are multiple layers of complexity in that space. Time may be the biggest factor. For top athletes, the window to excel is very small, and seizing that moment means everything. Payroll caps, free agency, the threat of arbitration, even trends like "money ball" are some of the many other factors at play. Like the levels of a video game, these challenges and nuances are what make me love what I do, and negotiating is at the heart of everything.

For 20 years I've negotiated contracts and branding deals for 300 clients, including top pro athletes, broadcasters, coaches such as Izzo, universities, manufacturers, and teams. Together, I've done probably more than $500 million in deals—from a record-setting "ball, shoe, glove" deal with Nike and appearances after a Hall of Fame induction in Cooperstown to a multimillion-dollar contract for John Smoltz and multiple contracts for Cy Young winners, all-stars, Hall of Famers, and Emmy Award–winning broadcasters. As one client remarked, "You could stack up all the contracts you have negotiated and walk right up 'em to the top of your office building."

None of the deals are linear, but neither is life. As a mother of three, I've negotiated deals while standing on the sidelines of my kids' soccer games. I've been in the heat of hopscotch when deals were closed, which isn't all that different from sitting at the head of a boardroom table— if you have your head in the right place. I buy pajamas with pockets for my cell phone but figured out how to tuck my phone into my wristband for even easier access. As with parenting or any deep relationship, negotiating well means always being ready. The most rewarding deals for me aren't the ones that are the most lucrative but the ones that change lives. I make 4 to 20 percent of what I negotiate, and so my family and I also bene-fit in real dollars when I bring a client the best deal possible. I've learned by watching great negotiators, understanding my own thresholds, and creating a systematic approach that pays off with consistent high-level results.

If you learn nothing else from me, know this: *effective negoti-ation is a conversation, a relationship,* a rhythm built over time. At the heart of my success is managing relationships well so that con-versations keep going, stay open, and spark more conversations, because the seeds of your next negotiation are planted in the one you are doing right now. A negotiation is a story, and good negotia-tors are like bestselling novelists who know the characters so well that nothing they do is surprising.

A negotiator studies the most important decision makers. He or she finds out their fears and desires, what they will give in to, and what they will not let go of without losing a part of themselves. Negotiating is more important than ever today as traditional business structures are disintegrating. We are more likely to negotiate for our own package deals than ever before. Even if you are with a long-term employer, you may find yourself negotiating to keep that job or for benefits such as flextime. Marriage is an ongoing negotiation, as is parenting. All your relationships are. Negotiations force you to communicate what is most important to you, and we all can be better at it.

No matter what level you are in your negotiations skills—whether you're a rookie or a major leaguer—your ability to have that conversation hinges on your grasp and consistent use of basic tools. These tools play out virtually the same way in every negotiation, and you need to keep them handy and sharp. In baseball, a five-tool player can field, throw, run, and hit for power and consistency. A great negotiator, I have seen time and time again, does these five things well:

1. Sets the Stage
2. Finds Common Ground
3. Asks with Confidence
4. Embraces the Pause
5. Knows When to Leave

As with a top baseball player, a negotiator's tools must become reflexive and instinctive. They have to be because in both worlds the window for action and success is narrow. Winning doesn't wait. Opportunity doesn't come around every day. To leverage and maximize these chances, you've got to be ready with multiple tools and the confidence to use them well. I wrote this book to share these tools with you so that you can learn from my mistakes and be conversant in the art of negotiation.

Now back to the closet. Why the closet? you ask. I needed to ground myself by finding a quiet spot where I could focus and speak from my heart without little ears to hear me. I ducked in there to collect myself and set the stage for success.

From my standpoint, we had worked hard for Izzo, too. We had set the stage by understanding his desires and motivations as much as possible and gleaning the same type of data from Kentucky. We helped him find common ground with Kentucky by showing him what the next step might look like and giving him information that would help him feel comfortable in that school's culture. That information included everything from the names on the athletic association board, especially its president, to schooling Izzo on all the current players and the team's upcoming schedule. We established what he would discuss and what he wouldn't. We asked with confidence to meet with the Kentucky athletic director after the tournament was over. We embraced the pause, that awkward time, as we waited for the other side to make the next move.

But here's the thing about negotiation: those steps are like waves on a beach. They repeat themselves over and over, especially in a big deal. They repeat between people who are negotiating and within negotiators themselves. The conversation is always going on.

In the closet, I knew that I had to reestablish common ground with Izzo. I had to go back at him after this pause. I had to be prepared to walk away. In our world, the verbal tirade he had just unleashed was a challenge. Was I going to take it? And if I did, would I be able to stand up for him the next time he entered negotiations?

At this crossroads, it wasn't just about me picking up the phone to make amends; it was a strategic move to reestablish respect, to recover the common ground that he had razed. That common ground had a shared language, and it wasn't one I wanted my young daughters to hear.

As soon as Izzo picked up, I started in, only to be interrupted.

"Why haven't you called me?" he said. "I have media calling me asking me what happened!"

"I don't like helping people who talk to me like you did the other night," I replied, practically snarling. "I don't get calls like the one from you the other night. I get thank you notes and flowers. Up and down my client list, there aren't any guys I care more about than you."

I kept going.

"No one has ever talked to me as you did. I'm not an eighteen-year-old in the huddle—I'm a coach that helps you win games, Tom. We were clear on what you wanted. But we both know in no way were you ready to 'walk there' or just say yes. We had more to discuss with them, and other guys didn't. Kentucky has an ego, and they couldn't have it hit the media again that another coach was not diving in. We might have tap-danced around the job for days. Kentucky wasn't about to let that happen."

There came another pause. Embrace it; don't fill it, I told myself. This is the power position, where things happen in negotiations.

Even in the silence, I felt he knew how much I cared.

"You're right," he finally said in a quiet voice. "I wasn't going to position myself like he [Gillispie] did. I didn't want to be in the middle of this. I'm a Spartan."

I love you, man, I thought to myself (heck, I'm a Michigan State alumna). I wasn't about to compromise his positioning or any of my clients'. His reputation, players, recruits—all of his stakeholders—would have blown up with the public fiasco that this would have become.

The call wasn't long, but it was powerful. It wasn't so much that I "won" but that we recovered our working relationship. Izzo remained my client. In many ways, what could have been the breaking point for our relationship became the turning point. We'll always be friends with a great respect for and trust in each other in part because of that experience. Each stage of every negotiation is a test of a relationship—and a chance to demonstrate your passion and character.

Trust is at the heart of negotiation and long-term success as a negotiator. The five tools are nothing without trust.

Billy Donovan is a great story about trust and misreading signs. We helped him move from a great college job at the University of Florida, where he had just won the national championship, to a great pro job at the Orlando Magic. He was ecstatic. So were we— until things quickly unraveled within just hours of his signing the new contract.

At seven-thirty the morning after announcing his move, Donovan informed us that he couldn't leave.

"I'm staying," he told us flatly, as if we could wave a magic wand and make six contracts go away (which we eventually did without any magic). In combing over my actions to better equip myself for the next deal, I asked myself what my priorities had been. Had we his agents been so focused on the terms of the contract that we hadn't spent any time negotiating with Billy? So often we assume that our clients understand the ramifications of their decisions, but that's not always true.

The trust that was broken when he went back on his decision was eventually recovered. We did a lot of patching up with the team Donovan rejected and resolved to take as much from this "failure" as we could.

We trusted that Donovan knew, beyond the papers and numbers of his contract, what this shift would look like down the road. We didn't ask, "What happens after two years if you don't win and you get fired?" In other words, could he reenter the college market and coach against Florida one day? Donovan was "the man" in Gainesville but wouldn't be in Orlando—and by the way, everyone in Gainesville would feel betrayed. Was he ready for this? We didn't ask.

We also misread a key relationship (Donovan and his athletic director) that pulled him back from the pro contract. After this fiasco, we made an even more concerted effort to look holistically at all of our clients, to study them as dynamic individuals, and to ask hard questions separate from our own financial interests. We got tougher at Setting the Stage and Finding Common Ground with our clients even before negotiating for them. Trust is easily broken, and building (and rebuilding) trust requires a lot of intentionality. You never know what you don't know, and assumptions kill a negotiation faster than anything else.

I take trust seriously even when my clients do not. Young ballplayers making seven-figure salaries are among the worst offenders. They tend to think that they will continue working at their elite level far longer than is possible statistically or otherwise. They often sign contracts without bothering to read the fine print. On some level, they believe nothing will stand in the way of their continued dominance of their field despite statistical and anecdotal evidence to the contrary. They trust me implicitly to give them a clean contract and help protect them. It's easy to see how these athletes have been taken advantage of in the past, because their default thinking is that nothing will change and they will always be on top of their game. I appreciate the trust on one level, but it's important to remind them that they must read and understand what they sign. Period.

In a space where trust is generally missing, there is a huge upside for the person who can stand in that gap and Find Common Ground. Most general managers, such as John Schuerholz of the Atlanta Braves, don't like agents. Yet when I bumped into him eating alone at a landmark Atlanta restaurant called Houston's, Schuerholz quickly invited me and my colleague to join him.

"I hate most agents," he remarked, "but I like you. I do." That comment helped my confidence and purpose soar. No matter how many times I broker a deal, the next negotiation is like trying the high dive for the first time. You put yourself on the line, and you can't assume that anyone has your back.

His comment also took me back to my days getting started in this business and how the five tools helped me establish trust and break into the field. I felt strongly that my firm needed to tap the deep baseball talent rising from our backyard, the suburbs of Atlanta. Georgia Tech had a good program, with players from Atlanta who seemed to mesh well with my firm's corporate values. The only problem was that I didn't know anyone on the Tech team. I had to meet them and persuade someone to take a chance on me even though I had never represented anyone as an agent.

The stage was set, and my common ground turned out to be the fence line where other agents stood. The difference was that I was there before every other agent and stayed after they all were gone. I literally "leaned in" to the fence, trying not to be too disgusted by the thick chaws of tobacco in the cheeks of other agents and scouts.

After getting to know a couple of players, I made my ask with as much confidence as I could muster. The first clients are the hardest, but with a few Tech players, I was in.

The other big lesson I learned in observing an array of college athletic programs was about the ethical boundaries to which some teams turn a blind eye. I could see what I would never do: illegal gifts such as wooden bats that some corrupt agents would "loan" to players and never request back. Some might have signatures from major leaguers, making those bats trophies that easily impressed college players. Or the wooden bats prepped them for summer ball in "The Cape," one of the proving grounds before the pro draft. Could I compete ethically in a space where the rules forbid even taking a player to dinner or buying him a Coke? For me, that question was answered with another: How can I not?

What grew out of this position was a greater resilience, because my sense of self and integrity did not waver with the changes around me. I had my anchor and held it, and my career grew. Resilience, I learned, is cherished by elite performers, because it separates them from the next level. The ability to bounce back from adversity allows you to achieve longevity, and that helps you build respect and trust.

Negotiation is more of an art than a science. Although Setting the Stage and Finding Common Ground can be quantified by numbers and statistics (and no negotiator should be without as much data as possible), the truly gifted negotiators display great intuition and instinct. Data is about the who, when, where, and what; intuition and art are about grasping the how and why. It's about the story and conversation, the power of intangibles in Asking with Confidence, Embracing the Pause, and Knowing When to Leave. Data gathering is like dating, getting to know someone and seeing if you might be interested. The other tools are more like marriage and parenting, requiring greater work and commitment but resulting in deep satisfaction.

WHERE ARE THE WOMEN?

What I didn't see much on my journey through the sports world was other women negotiating. This intrigued me, and so did the research about what keeps women from claiming their place at the negotiating table. More than men, women avoid the chaos and ambiguity of negotiation. They buy into beliefs, expectations, and stereotypes of women being ineffective in this arena. One motivation for writing this book is to encourage women to develop 360-Degree Awareness, my term for embracing and observing all the aspects of a new industry, client, or challenge. This awareness builds an appetite for ambiguity and more fluidity in a changing environment. I call this being an authentic chameleon.

You don't have to lose your femininity to negotiate effectively. Every woman should recognize the factors at play for her that most men don't see. That's just smart preparation.

ON YOUR OWN TERMS

Negotiation is most successful when the terms are clear and specific to everyone involved. That's true in the smallest words that we use. When we talk about who we are negotiating with, *the other side* is simply that: another perspective. I prefer *side* to *opponent*. Side suggests a location, which is important as we talk about common ground.

Remember the blind side? The side is one way of looking at the whole. In the old days, baseball teams were called sides; golf rounds were scores of the front side and back side. Sides are part of a complete shape, and the shape of negotiation is defined by give-and-take, ebb and flow.

If it's all one side, then there is no negotiation. Negotiations have to have sides, but they don't have to be automatically opposi-tional. Think of a prism having sides and exploding into a rainbow when the light hits it just so. Great negotiators find and grasp as many sides as they can.

THE FIRE WITHIN

As a society, we like to label and brand people, and so we pigeon-hole them as natural talents or born losers, as if willpower played no part in brain development. I'll share a personal story that I hope will encourage you to keep an open mind about your innate gifts and your ability to work toward being as good a negotiator as you can be.

My mom was a schoolteacher and speech pathologist; my dad, a pharmaceutical rep. I'm not sure if what I have was inherited from them or learned, but from a young age, I saw the way my par-ents did things and knew I wanted to follow their lead.

We were a middle-class family in Michigan, and Mom and Dad loved getting a deal or discount. They knew which places had "kids eat free night," and when we went out, we knew to order only water; a Sprite or Coke was out of the question as an expensive luxury. On many occasions I watched Mom talk the grocery store cashier into accepting an expired coupon. If she was unsuccessful, I saw the item go back on the shelf. Over time I could see that her method wasn't all that different from the way Dad brokered a deal for Mich-igan State football tickets from a scalper in the stadium parking lot. He knew the best time to get the best deal (close to kickoff) and when to walk away. Mom and Dad were also big givers, Mom espe-cially. She donated hundreds of hours as a community leader.

What they taught me was what they had learned from their parents. My dad's dad worked on the assembly line at the big Chrysler plant on Detroit's south side. Mom's parents were chicken farmers who were successful enough to have the first car in their town. Margins were slim, and they all had a sense that they never knew what tomorrow would bring. Working hard and saving was a given, and even today Mom can tell you the price of milk at multiple grocery stores. They didn't hire for services my brothers and I could do. I mowed the lawn. My brothers had paper routes.

All their tiny negotiations added up over time and paid off when my parents were able to buy a house in the same neighborhood as couples who had had much more lucrative careers. Izzo lived around the corner, as did professional hockey players, business owners, and retired doctors. I'm immensely proud of what my family stands for and proudly say that the fundamentals of my negotiating skills began with them.

So whether you are haggling over a grocery coupon or a multi-million-dollar contract, you're engaged in a critical conversation. The more comfortable you are with that conversation, the better your results will be. My five tools will build that comfort for success, building trust in yourself and trust from others. They will give you the guts to negotiate.

Let's go!

1

Setting the Stage

Nate McMillan was one of the best defensive players in the history of the National Basketball Association. When he retired from the Seattle Supersonics, he was the team's all-time leader in assists and steals. He was all over the ball in every game for what seemed like forever: the NBA has one of the longest seasons in pro sports, and he thrived for a dozen years. McMillan was a grinder, and that work ethic and success made him a natural to become a popular coach for Seattle, too. Talk about someone with his head in the game.

He's also a dad with two children, Jamelle and Brittany Michelle. One night he was all over them. "Get in bed!" Nate was bellowing. The kids weren't having any of it, but he was putting his foot down. It was a school night, right?

"Dad, it's Saturday night!" they shouted.

"Get in bed!" he yelled, and a long pause stretched out between them.

We teased McMillan about this incident and then laughed, because in a way it's a tribute to his dedication to his sport. His story, though, brings up something that is important for you to be aware of in negotiation. The first tool in negotiating is knowing exactly where you stand.

You'd be surprised at how many people don't know the basic facts—the equivalent of what day it is—when they enter into a deal. This is as simple and as hard as it sounds. It's simple because it means knowing exactly what you want and what the other side wants and who will be making the decision for the other side (the point person). It's hard because truly knowing the details of a deal requires drilling as deep as you can get, the way lawyers do when they prepare for court. They don't want to be blindsided by an answer from a witness or information admitted into court that they didn't know was coming.

Setting the Stage means doing your homework and, when you think you've done it all, finding more to do. Being prepared is half the work of negotiating. Sometimes it's more than 50 percent. Data, facts, and observations, even intuition and gut feelings that you make note of, are where you have to start. If you're a numbers junkie, love to collect trivia, and enjoy looking up the etymology of obscure words, this tool will come naturally to you. If you're not into research, you will find some help in this book on ways to approach this necessary step with imagination and enthusiasm. Negotiations depend on Setting the Stage.

360-DEGREE AWARENESS

Your best shot at successful negotiation is establishing what I call 360-Degree Awareness. This isn't merely a matter of paying attention, though that's where it starts. It means that your vision extends from your world into the spheres of those most important to your current negotiation.

Attaining 360-Degree Awareness starts by knowing the goals, needs, gaps, values, and fears of the other side so that your actions can parallel where they are or will be as the negotiation unfolds.

A great example of the power of this level of awareness occurred when we negotiated sports broadcaster Erin Andrews's second contract with ESPN. In that world, sideline reporters are plentiful, and ESPN doesn't pay them well because it doesn't have to. There's always another pretty face with hungry ambition who will work for less.

Erin's heart wasn't totally at ESPN. I knew that not by her admission but from my sense, and you probably know it too if you saw her on *Dancing with the Stars*, the reality show in which celebrities compete with professional dancers in a ballroom dance competition. I understood why Erin wanted to go Hollywood, but when we discussed her contract negotiations with ESPN, she didn't have the awareness she needed to understand what she was giving up by pursuing entertainment and reality shows. Unlike athletes, who can be very insecure and worried that everything is going to end suddenly if they are injured or cut from a team, Erin felt that she could stay in sports and should make more money from ESPN— more than the $200,000 or so a year that someone in her position as a sideline commentator pulls down. Weren't more people watching the network because of her reality show popularity? Shouldn't she set the comps now?

That wasn't the perception, or the reality, for ESPN. The talent is secondary to the product: the heroes on the field. The network does not place great value on the people with mikes on the sidelines and in the booths. ESPN's position is that the network has made the talent who they are, so why would any of the talent want to leave or expect a better stage anywhere else? At the time, except for the rare crossover personality such as Robin Roberts, who left ESPN and ended up on ABC, TV sports personalities had very little latitude in what they did and how long they did it for. My 360-Degree Awareness took into consideration Erin's popularity as a sizable factor in her contract negotiation, but it wasn't the advantage she thought it was.

From my perspective, she didn't have more leverage, she had less, because ESPN didn't know in which direction her commitment was going. As our talks continued over Erin's salary, I was very surprised at the level of comfort ESPN seemed to have with walking away from her. In the network's view, Hollywood took time away from the homework she had to complete to be current on the grapevine in college sports; that's a lot more work than fans realize. A bigger question was identity. Her job required her to grab coaches on the field for key interviews at halftime and at the close of a game. As I did with Izzo, she often had to clear the emotional field with those guys and command their respect. Because they were now used to seeing her in a sleek low-cut dress and ballroom high heels, could she still command professional respect from those who mattered? These coaches are still for the most part old school guys who see women in traditional roles. In short, ESPN doubted she could be good at both performing and reporting, and so there remained a sizable gap between what she thought she should earn and what the other side thought she could deliver.

It was the right move for us to stay friends but for her to find another agent: someone who danced in both spaces, whose firm had both athletes and entertainers. My firm didn't. As Erin embraced entertainment as much as or more than sports, we hugged and promised to stay connected. Representing Erin taught me the power of striving for the greatest awareness of the factors in a negotiation. Before you make your optimal move, you have to know where you stand. She later inked a contract for a significant salary with Fox and has become a fabulous crossover personality.

A far less glitzy example of 360-Degree Awareness occurred on a recent flight from Atlanta to Phoenix. I had rushed to board, taking my seat with a huge appetite and some anxiety. I had been eating like a health nut and saw myself getting trapped in a small space for hours with no decent food.

Because my work takes me across the country regularly and I try to upgrade my seat whenever possible, I was thrilled to discover that a meal was being served where I was sitting in first class. But what kind of food? When I asked, the attendant told me that the options were chicken salad (which I love) and pasta (which I don't eat).

Prior knowledge helped me Set the Stage: I knew that the presence of chicken salad on the menu didn't mean I would actually get chicken salad. On even-numbered flights, the crew would serve meals from the front row, where I sat in 1B, to the back row. On odd-numbered flights like this one to Phoenix, the meals would be served in the opposite direction, meaning I would get the tail end of the choices.

"Can I ask you a favor?" I said with a warm tone to the attendant, and then explained my situation and where my seat was. "Think I can get a chicken salad?"

"Sure, you got it," he replied.

When they got to my row, pasta was all that was left. Everyone around me might have been OK with not having a choice; I was happy to have thought ahead to ask them to save me what I could eat, and to practice on a small scale a skill that is critical when the stakes get high. "I got you covered, Ms. Fletcher," the other attendant said as she served my chicken salad.

One airplane meal doesn't mean much; my point is that when you are 360-Degree Aware, you can stay a step ahead or a beat ahead, and that can help your chances of achieving your negotiating objective.

KNOW YOUR COMPARABLES

The foundation of 360-Degree Awareness is a statistic called a comparable. A comp is simply the amount that is being paid for a similar service or product. The most common form of a comp is in real estate. To price or estimate the value of a house, Realtors seek out the final sale prices of houses that are of similar size and location. Comps are a baseline for negotiating; numbers and specificity automatically convey authority. Assume that the other side will know them; if they do not, that's an obvious advantage for you.

The agent business isn't as straightforward as real estate. Sure, we can find comparable salaries for coaches at public universities; that's on public record. But negotiating on behalf of a coach is not just about salary. There's almost always something at stake besides money. A simple example is that a big-time college coach is going to have a country club membership. The cost of joining a private club isn't typically on public record, but it's an important piece of a contract that we need to find. Shoe deals are also more challenging. Car deals and apparel deals live in contracts today. Maybe the former coach is a friend and can provide some insight. Finding out comps can involve building trust with the gatekeepers and sources of that information. Agents don't collaborate, and so getting information from other agents isn't an option. Other times it comes straight to me thanks to a well-worded Google alert. You've got to know what information you need, how to get it, and how to make sure it's airtight. Only then are you fully prepared for negotiating.

Here are some other sources for comps:

- Any third parties who have worked with you and the other side

- Your colleagues who have negotiated or worked in this space

- People who used to work for the other side or in this industry
- Marketing research
- News reports
- The other side's website

For instance, with a major league baseball player, we Set the Stage primarily by understanding the team's options, payroll, free agents, and minor league prospects. Was it a moneyball team, eking out wins with players who specialized at getting on base? Setting the Stage means I am not just understanding the team a little but sitting in its chair in spirit and getting into its head, its heart, its staff, its manager, and its trustees. We study its needs and current roster and look at the corresponding position players who possess the same level of service and similar stats. The market dictates comparables that can support (or sometimes not support) your case.

The point of comps is to find similarities, but often when I represent an athlete or someone else in the sports world, comps are just a starting point for what makes my client distinct—or what does not. One of my favorite broadcasters, Ernie Johnson, Jr., mans an anchor booth with two former NBA players. During the league's superlong season, he is the relatively bland filling in a celebrity sandwich of former NBA star Kenny Smith and larger-than-life talker Charles Barkley.

Barkley is an extraordinary personality who is beyond enthusiastic about saying the first thing that comes to mind. More often than not, his ad-libs are creative and hilarious, worth tuning in for even when the games are lackluster. EJ, in contrast, is dialed way back. Compared with Barkley, he's practically wallpaper. But Barkley is Barkley only because EJ and Smith excel at playing supporting roles. They help rein him in because the network wants Barkley to be a loose cannon just short of offending viewers. Its gives him just the right amount of rope: enough to make fans tune in but not enough to hang himself. Say Barkley is making $15 million; that's not that relevant to EJ. Ernie has won two Emmys, is competitive with a pool of great broadcasters, and is still making a great salary; Barkley is one of a kind, virtually in his own pool. He is going to have more leverage, and the comps we use for EJ's deal are going to include analysts and play-by-play guys from other networks.

THE SPERM CLUB: EVERYONE HAS A STORY

I negotiated contracts for Major League Baseball analyst Chip Caray. He's the third generation of his family to star in this business—after his grandfather Harry Caray called Chicago Cubs games and his father, Skip Caray, worked the booth for the Atlanta Braves. Chip had the benefit of "the Sperm Club" in finding his way into broadcasting, which is so competitive that he wouldn't have lasted long if he didn't have the chops. (EJ, who called the Atlanta Braves games for several seasons in the mid-1990s with his dad, Ernie Johnson, Sr., is in the Sperm Club, too.) The Sperm Club is a good reminder to me that every client has his or her own story that is separate from the comps. Sometimes the story can be even more important than the comps, and so it's important to have both in your pocket.

In Chip's case, I know that he has had to work harder than most because he has had to overcome the expectations stemming from his last name. Perhaps because of this challenge, Chip loves to work. He has his own style, preparation, and relationships. He loves to call games. He would do it every day. In his contract, I always tried to get him a minimum number of games and then a per-game rate for additional games. This type of contract was always working in his favor because he loves to pick up as many games as possible. I have also learned that these types of contracts are the ones I have the most faith in for my clients. They are all so competitive that less of a base salary gives them a chance to bet on their own success. How much do they believe in themselves? Long-term deals offer security, that's for certain, but successful athletes are that way because they perform so well during chaos and anxiety points of games. I want to craft a deal that will allow their competitive juices to flourish, because that is the engine that has gotten them to this point. Why change it?

Negotiating the best deal for Chip was fairly easy after we got clear on what would best motivate him. You can't assume it's what would motivate you or anyone else.

WHAT IS YOUR WHY?

One of the main drivers of any negotiation is the why. This goes to the heart of your motivation: your fear or desire surrounding a deal. It's critical to know your why. Washington Redskins quarterback Robert Griffin III—or RG3, as the young superstar is known—was a rookie at the 2012 Redskins training camp who had all the media clamoring for an interview. A local reporter noticed a simple statement posted on his locker: "KNOW YOUR WHY."

"What's that about?" he asked Griffin.

Griffin explained that each team member has to know his why and the why of the guys around him. If you have a why, he said, you are more willing to sacrifice for those around you because you know their purpose.

Know your why is a powerful step toward clarity. Although it seems simple, how many of us ask it of ourselves and can articulate the answer? In terms of negotiating, why are you doing this deal?

(In terms of work, you could ask yourself why you spend 82,000 hours doing it. That is how many hours the average person works after college until retirement.) If you aren't clear on the why, those 82,000 hours and any negotiation will be slow and painful.

If you need a reminder, take a cue from RG3. Put a sticky note on your desk that reminds you to "KNOW YOUR WHY." Clarity will follow.

THE INNER BASELINE

The relationship with EJ points out another aspect of Setting the Stage: as I try to find the baseline for my client's value, I'm also looking to understand the values inside him or her. I want to know what beyond money or status—the obvious elements—will make my client satisfied, at the very least. More than that, I want him or her to be blown away. Knowing these values gives us more choices, and more choices always create a better platform for negotiation.

I know what a good salary does for EJ. When I meet him for lunch, his severely disabled son Michael joins us. Michael uses a wheelchair, and a good salary for EJ means Michael uses a great wheelchair. EJ is terrific at what he does, and what is at stake for him is taking care of his family, and the wheelchair is a big part of that. Each week EJ goes to the grocery store and always stops to buy a bouquet for Cheryl, his wife, and always buys an extra bouquet. As he leaves the store, he looks for the right stranger to give those flowers to. Who knows how many regular folks have been blessed by EJ's flowers? There's no telling, but these bouquets bring him so much joy. As his agent, I look for these details. These are part of his inner baseline. Take away his ability to get the wheelchair or buy the flowers—which, granted, may not be a lot in terms of dollars—and his life has a lot less joy.

As I do my homework and Set the Stage for negotiating, I want to know as much as I can about the side I am representing. I want to know what makes up my client's inner baseline. I have my own inner baseline too. Because EJ's values align so closely with my own, I love being a part of his negotiations. Ensuring a fair salary and compensation for him is fun for me. I know he's not going to go sideways for a couple of thousand dollars extra. Sure, I can help a client who I know is going to spend his paycheck on strip clubs and fancy purses, but I have a greater heart for EJ and the clients whose drive is to do good in the world. When he wins the John Wooden Keys to Life Award given to individuals who live out faith, integrity, and character, I'm beyond thrilled. His professional platform is all about him being a great role model in life. I know that his heart is not about the money but the message, and we stayed clear on that from the front end and consistently throughout the contract negotiation.

Knowing my inner baseline has been integral to my success. Without ethics, anything can happen. You might succeed in the short term, but in the long term, I believe that skirting ethics is a losing game. Over time, building trust is what the game is about, and in a small world such as pro sports, people talk. Trust transfers. Deals get done more quickly and better with trust. When you are unethical or untrustworthy, when you cut corners and fail to follow up, that reputation spreads fast, especially through social media. Protecting this inner baseline is a constant priority for me as a negotiator.

Competition rules the sports world. The numbers can get so inflated that what matters, especially to many top coaches, is that they make a penny more than the next guy. I've seen contracts that require a team to pay a coach one dollar more than the highest paid coach in the league. Negotiating on their behalf is not about money; it's about the extra edge that represents a bigger value that is close to their hearts. Thus, although the extra penny is quantitative, what it represents is abstract. It's these intangibles that a great negotiator must pinpoint, absorb, and practically embody. A great example of this occurred when Peyton Manning joined the Denver Broncos. When asked why he had chosen Denver, Manning said it was all about a relationship with his hero John Elway, a Broncos executive who had competed well into his mid-thirties just as Manning was doing. "Elway's gift for reconciling Manning the football player and Manning the human being may very well have been the tiebreaker," observed Yahoo! sportswriter Doug Farrar. "While Elway sees the greatest quarterback ever to play the game in Manning's past, present and future, he can also do the same by looking in the mirror. [Elway] could look Manning square in the eye . . . tell him what his remaining career could be through personal experience, and complete the sale with no hype and nothing but the truth." Making a legacy was what drove this negotiation. The salary was almost an afterthought.

Therefore, as we collect the comps that relate to a deal, I am mindful of not just the numbers but what the numbers represent. Personality is another big factor. I hope that a major league player who locks in a multimillion-dollar salary is going to relax because the deal represents security no matter how he plays. The guy whose salary sets a record has to have ice in his veins. At the end of the bell curve on deals, you can move into enormous pressure. If he doesn't deliver, the heat in the clubhouse from his teammates who are making a fraction of his paycheck is tremendous. Any slump can spiral into absolute misery. I'd be the first in line to help the guy max the contract, but it's also my duty to Set the Stage with him on what those expectations will mean. If he ends up miserable from some aspect of the deal that I could have warned him about, he might just go looking for another agent. If I want to keep him happy, I need to be brutally honest about the intangibles.

If you can do both—research the data and understand what they represent in the abstract—your actions in the heat of negotiation will be more authentic, and you'll end up with a much more productive result.

VALUING YOUR ASSETS

My clients who are professional golfers represent a great lens into the importance of understanding what resources enabled you to get to the point of negotiation and remind you to never forget those resources. Having 360-Degree Awareness means that you've taken stock not just of what you are worth in the market (through comps) but of what your assets mean to your success so far. Those resources can sometimes become a point of negotiation.

When John Smoltz, the great veteran pitcher for the Atlanta Braves, was rehabbing with one of the team's farm clubs in Greenville, South Carolina, he took along his son Andrew, who was barely in middle school. In the sixth inning, Smoltz couldn't find his glove. He couldn't find Andrew either.

When Smoltz finally tracked him down, Andrew told him how he had made some new friends by selling them Smoltz's glove for $10.

"You gotta be kidding me," Smoltz hollered at his son. "Here's a ball. I'll sign it for them if they give me back my glove!"

Andrew did get it back. I always laugh thinking that John was playing baseball under a multimillion-dollar contract, and his son was selling a necessary piece of his success for only $10 at a minor league ballpark. The story also reveals that the closer you are to someone in a negotiation, the less value you see in that person.

This is important to keep in mind for the later chapters in which I emphasize the importance of keeping your emotions in check through the negotiation process.

Here's another great example of the importance of valuing your assets as you Set the Stage for a deal. Pro golfers depend on great equipment that feeds their confidence. Equipment manufacturers often dangle big money in front of a great player to entice him or her to switch equipment. We're going to bring great deals to our clients as a matter of course, but we like to Set the Stage on what deals they might be most open to, such as equipment contracts. Two clients from rival colleges took different routes.

Matt Kuchar, who graduated from Georgia Tech, could have made double or triple his equipment contract if he'd opted to switch from Bridgestone. But we knew and respected the fact that he did not want to switch. He had made this clear from our first meeting, when he was interviewing us because he wanted to switch agents. The details of that day illustrate how I try to Set the Stage in such situations.

Matt had yet to win a PGA Tour event when I greeted him at the elevator doors that opened right into the office. He looked rich: gray slacks, a royal blue alligator belt, and conservative-looking blue shoes with a gray cashmere zip-up pullover. This first impression held true as I learned over time that he is a reserved, deliberate, even-tempered, intelligent guy. He holds power from being tough to read.

In the boardroom, his facial expression told me he wasn't sure where to sit. Setting the Stage can mean offering a taste of what a successful deal will taste like. Here was a classic opportunity for an appetizer.

"You are the CEO," I said, pointing to the head of the table. "Sit there."

After just a few minutes to discuss Georgia Tech sports, I got right to the point. The meeting was to discuss his expectations of an agent and for us to present our pitch: the why, how, and what we would do if we represented him.

"Tell me a little bit about your current situation," I opened.

He demurred, preferring not to give us much so that he could get a raw pitch. "He just doesn't have great relationships in the market," was all he said.

Perfect, I thought. That's what I can do with confidence for him all day. We talked about what we might go for, such as deals for shoes, gloves, and what amounts to billboard space on the sleeve, yoke, and collar of his shirt. We discussed his interest in outings with corporate executives, his schedule, his travel, even issues such as ticket requests and golf teachers if needed. Matt listened intently with little reaction, as if he had heard it all before, but he was intrigued.

"You're with Bridgestone now. You like their stuff?" I asked.

"I do," he replied.

"They service you well?"

"Yes, very."

In that opening meeting in which we Set the Stage with Matt, this conversation helped us understand that he wanted to focus on playing and winning golf tournaments with the clubs and balls that felt the most comfortable. The meeting lasted about an hour, and the next day Matt delivered an executed contract. We had Set the Stage for understanding him well, both due to our meeting and in light of various mutual connections.

He knew he would be happy with us, and his stellar career as one of the leading players on the PGA Tour proves that his choice was right for him. We would jump in to negotiate on his behalf for contract extensions with Bridgestone but not try to attract new equipment companies.

Nick Cassini, from the University of Georgia, in contrast, played Titleist irons all through high school and college. They worked awesomely; he led Georgia to an NCAA championship, and in his senior year he won conference player of the year and a berth on the team for the Walker Cup, a prestigious competition for the best American and British amateurs. He was ranked number one in the country.

After graduating, he chose an agent who promised him, "We are so confident you will get a large equipment deal that we'll give you $250,000. When the deal is secured, we'll capture the first $250 plus our fee and the rest goes to you." Nick needed the money, and so he agreed. Well, guess what the agent was worried about now? Not ensuring that Nick was comfortable with the equipment but getting him the most lucrative equipment deal possible so that agent could recoup his money.

Nick switched from Titleist, and whether it was physical or mental, he couldn't find a golf hole for years. He also struggled with injuries. I had sent him a condolence card when his grandfather died, bought some art that I really liked from his mom at an art show, and genuinely stayed connected. He knew that my focus was ensuring that he was armed with the tools to win tournaments; that was more important than cash advances. Soon he called me and asked me to be his agent.

I worked on getting him exemptions to compete at the tournaments and venues where he was most comfortable. Ultimately, he wasn't able to come back from the equipment setback and other obstacles to his pro career, which was unfortunate. It's a story that shows that every person involved in a negotiation has different motivations. An agent is going to push for the equipment deal because that's where he or she makes money. The agent isn't getting a cut of the prize money. I'm not sure that pro golfers always think about what motivates an agent to pitch an equipment deal. The golfer must always weigh the offer against the familiarity of the equipment that got him or her this far.

What I saw far too often was young athletes whose bulletproof mindset had gotten them this far, and they figured it would overcome any adversity that life threw at them. As Nick told a reporter later, "When you play golf and that's all you've done, you don't know what else is out there. You kind of have this notion that I'm a golfer and that's it." When adversity struck, not many of them could adequately surf it; they hadn't really thought it could happen to them, because nothing bad ever had. That impermeable mindset was their greatest strength as an athlete and a big, big weakness as a negotiator. This lack of awareness—blindness, really—can be true for anyone, not just athletes.

THE POWER OF DETAILS

I cannot say enough about the need to nail down the details in this stage of negotiating. Another way to look at 360-Degree Awareness is as seeing what is at stake through a different lens. When I look at EJ with my wide lens, I see that he wants to do good in the world. With a telephoto lens, I see the flowers and a wheelchair. My success in negotiating has come from observing, absorbing, and delivering on the details that matter to my clients.

Another example is Mike Fratello, who was a coach for the Cleveland Cavaliers. He was fine with the multimillion-dollar contract we negotiated for him, but it didn't include a service that he really wanted: dry cleaning. Like most top NBA coaches, Mike loves to coach in a great-looking suit, and those clothes take a pounding on the sidelines. What we worked out for Mike was a "trade out" with a Cleveland dry cleaner in which he would promote that business in return for free dry cleaning. The deal was done with the same fervor as a $29 million contract even though trade outs brought me no income. The cleaner loved it because it got lots of fans coming to its store. Mike loved it because it was "free" to him, and like other clients, he loved not having to pay.

It's been eye-opening to me how many elite people in sports who have plenty of cash to spend get such a rush out of a freebie (even if it's only perceived as free—after all, Fratello did have to make a public appearance at the dry cleaner). No matter how much cash an athlete makes in a contract, what he or she seems to get most excited about is the free stuff, the gear or car, in exchange for an appearance. What I see in their eyes is the excitement of the deal itself. It's the same look I get when I go to a discount clothing store and buy a $100 dress for $50.

As I Set the Stage for a deal, I look for bonuses that will make their eyes light up, that make them know I have them completely covered. By understanding these details and delivering some swag, I show how much I care. Don't underestimate the power of swag, whatever that amounts to in your business or industry.

Another point is to *get it in writing*. Tom Izzo, the Michigan State basketball coach, gives each of his players a 3-by-5 card at the beginning of the season. On it, each of them answers this question: "What do you want out of this season?" Then he meets with each player to discuss his goals. If the goal is a national championship, Izzo might say, "Great, to have a national championship, we are going to have to hustle each and every day. So it's okay with you that if I see you not hustling, I will hold you accountable to me regarding this goal?" Or, again in an encouraging tone, "I see you want to graduate with honors. So if I find out you're skipping class, it's okay with you to hold you accountable, right? As your coach, your leader, that's my role in this, right?"

Izzo is Setting the Stage in writing, and this step gives him the trust and credibility to rip into his players on the sideline as a way of focusing them on the task and clearing away all distractions. He is merely holding them accountable, minute by minute, on the basis of what each of them wrote for him. It's not hard for him to ask them to dig deep, because they've essentially asked him, way before the chaos kicked in, to do precisely that. He has clarity and accountability because he has Set the Stage well, and that's a big reason why he wins.

In contrast, not having this kind of accountability is one reason so many pro athletes end up broke or in debt despite a trajectory of great wealth early in their careers. They have no one around them with the guts to say, "No, we're not going to buy that car." They have no one who can go up to them and tell them, "You make $500,000 every other week. That is not normal. It's not going to last forever." They have no one they respect enough to listen to or no one who is willing to walk the tightrope that could lose him the business but demonstrate his true desire to protect the athlete.

It's like when I had to teach my kids that a debit card is not a magic trick that substitutes for paying. They need a reality check when they say, "Just use that thing, Mommy," for a toy or something they think they need. Accountability usually brings pain. That is part of the maturing process. Often you have to feel pain for honesty to work, and this is the work of Setting the Stage as well. It's not as simple as it first looks and can sometimes be downright difficult.

Setting the Stage is also about establishing communication, which is a basis for all trust. It almost seems impossible that this happened, but Tarell Brown, who played cornerback for the San Francisco 49ers, lost out on $2 million because his agent didn't tell him he had to work out with the team during the off-season. He forfeited that money by going home to Texas. He fired his agent for not telling him about that part of the contract, and his next agent had to try to talk the team into giving him part of the money anyway.

A LESSON IN HOMEWORK: DOC RIVERS

Glenn "Doc" Rivers had been a great NBA player and broadcaster, and we had done a TV deal for him that had him working 25 days a year. That arrangement, though, wasn't working for his wife and four kids (one son, Austin, now plays in the NBA, but this was when he was still at home).

Doc's wife, Kris, called one day when we were at spring training. "You have got to get him a job," she said flatly. "He's driving everyone crazy." She chuckled, but she meant it.

Fast-forward past us getting him back in the NBA coaching ranks with Orlando. Doc ended up at the Boston Celtics, guiding them to a world championship in 2008. Coaches sweat and pray for an NBA championship ring, and Doc's road to that moment started with his wife's desperate call.

She Set the Stage for us to negotiate on his behalf. Then he Set the Stage for himself. He didn't have to have a coaching job; he went into negotiations interviewing a team as much as the team interviewed him. Doc did his homework about why the previous coach didn't work out and what the expectations of him would be. He called the players and got clear with the general manager and the team owner on questions such as these:

- What's broken with the current team?
- Who controls draft picks and trades?
- What are the ownership's goals?
- Are the expectations realistic?
- Who can be trusted and who can't?

These types of questions help Set the Stage. Any question will help you gain knowledge about the other side, even it's as simple as "How are you doing?" or "How's your family?" Sure, they can give you a throwaway "Fine," but you still want to listen and observe. Nonverbals offer the majority of data for the most successful negotiators and salespeople.

Much of my career has been built doing all this for people who could not (or chose not to) do it for themselves. Not only did they have to trust me, but I had to trust myself. I quickly learned that some great athletes and coaches Set the Stage better than others. One guy who comes to mind is Joe Theismann, the great Washington Redskins quarterback, a Super Bowl winner, an All-American at Notre Dame, and the NFL's Man of the Year for his community service.

It's instructive to observe people who make great transitions in their lives, because those skills are useful in negotiating as well. Joe made a great transition into life after football because he looked past the glory of his 12-year NFL career to what was next. He honed other skills as a public speaker and entrepreneur. He combed through the TV contracts that we did with him like few other clients. I admired his methodical nature and his grasp of concepts such as indemnification. He is a deliberate and bright individual, and that paved the way to his success after football.

Foresight is imperative for Setting the Stage. It's like a great chess player seeing possible moves and outcomes that will lead to capturing the opponent's king.

THE RIGHT TRIGGER PERSON

Setting the Stage means knowing who is going to make the decision for the other side and who is going to be the biggest influence on the other side. It's not always who you think it is.

One of my tougher deals was for Jeff Francoeur, the phenomenal right fielder and hometown hero for the Atlanta Braves. Like all young players, he spent his first three years making the league minimum salary. Knowing the Braves would tender him a new contract, we gathered data and comps on negotiating for what would be a significant raise on the basis of his accomplishments and trajectory. Jeff was eager to get paid the most he could and believed he would prevail in the free agent bargaining system, which can be a crapshoot because of arbitration. He pushed for very specific base numbers and bonuses.

We Set the Stage for negotiating his contract, hoping to avoid arbitration. Arbitration is a process we must enter if we fail to negotiate with the team for a one-year or multiyear deal by a designated date. I felt that arbitration represented a failure, because someone else who wasn't as close to our client (the arbitrator) would be solving an issue for which I felt we were responsible. Also, arbitration is all or nothing. Either we get what we want or the team does. Arbitration also forces the player to hear the team's criticism of him as its way of lowering the number. I didn't think Jeff needed to hear any of that. I was as tough as I had ever been in a contract, knowing what we were up against.

With the goal of avoiding arbitration, I began discussing the deal with the Braves' front office on a Tuesday. The assistant to the assistant general manager told me he would be making the decision. I didn't believe him, but at that point I didn't have another choice. He was the Braves' representative. The conversations were not substantive that day, and I quickly began to realize that he wasn't the trigger guy. He was simply trying to be the hero and tough guy for the team.

By the evening, his boss, the assistant general manager, called me and said he would be the one making the decision. "If you and

I can't get it done, we will see you in Phoenix at arbitration hearings," he told me. I still didn't believe him. This was all stage setting. My side stayed firm in our position and continued asking questions about how and why the team had arrived at its numbers.

Pinpointing the authority to commit is a common problem for negotiators, and asking questions helps provide clarity and uncover a web of other stakeholders who may influence and even decide how the deal will go. John Gasink, who teaches negotiation at West Point, and Jeff Weiss, a former consultant on negotiation to Fortune 500 companies, have written about this. The other side isn't just negotiating with you; it's negotiating with its colleagues, supervisors, and others who want to know (and second-guess) the deal you are trying to make. Basically you are looking at the other side as a slice of bread, but in reality there's a whole big sandwich there that you need to dissect.

In the article "The 'Other' Party: Getting into the Mind of Your Negotiating Counterpart," Gasink and Weiss write, "Without knowing the other party's level of authority (e.g., ability to commit to an entire deal, ability to commit to parts of a deal, no ability to commit but tasked with exploring possibilities at the table) and with whom—if anyone—they have to negotiate internally, it is very difficult to negotiate with them in an effective, efficient manner. Furthermore, many negotiators use ambiguity about their authority as a negotiation tactic—they negotiate a deal that their counterpart thinks is complete, then come back to the table and say that although they are in favor of the deal, their boss (or approval group) needs a few more things included or improved before giving sign off."

As the Francoeur negotiation got closer to the wire, to the date by which we would go to arbitration, the trigger person changed once again. I'll save the rest of the story for a later chapter because it relates to another tool. Just remember that the other side isn't always who you first think it is.

DON'T MAKE ASSUMPTIONS

It's so easy to think that you and the other side know what each other is thinking, because it is so obvious in your own mind. This has even been the subject of research that showed that what we think of as our transparency is often an illusion and that the other side doesn't pick up on nearly as much as we think it does. The bottom line is that assumptions are dangerous; clarity is everything.

I'll never forget sitting in a boardroom on a pretty day with someone who reminds me a lot of Doc Rivers. Bright and articulate, Clark Kellogg is a basketball analyst who is also a good father and husband. CBS basketball coverage benefits from how much coaches and athletes trust him. He has a lot of sources who will talk to him off the record, and that's extremely valuable to a network. All that made him perfect for an even higher-profile position.

"Have you ever considered being a coach?" I asked Clark, and it seemed like a softball question. Clark connects with everyone; why wouldn't he want to make 5 or 10 times what someone in the media makes?

"I just don't want that kind of family life," Clark said. His daughter was playing volleyball at a nearby college. He wanted more time with her and the rest of his family at this stage in his life. This conversation got me clear on what made him tick and how much work he wanted to do. I would never act on the assumption that he wanted to be a coach; these simple questions are a safeguard measure in Setting the Stage to get clear on both short- and long-term goals.

It's really easy to assume, and the easiest way to observe this is when someone doesn't bother to ask questions. I saw this failure time and time again with financial advisors. They would show up at an appointment with an athlete, coach, or broadcaster and just start talking, pulling out pie charts and their bios and making a pitch on why our client needed their help. What would have been so much more effective would have been to start by asking a couple of questions out of the gate such as, "What are you looking for in a financial advisor?" and, "Who taught you about money?" What if one of the few sentences they used as a pitch was "I am here to help you protect your wealth"? That would have been so much more effective and efficient for everyone.

Asking questions is the mark of an authentic chameleon, someone who is always trying to discover a way he or she can connect in a particular situation and adapt to do that in an authentic way.

One of the foremost researchers in the field of negotiation, Professor Leigh Thompson at the Kellogg School of Business at Northwestern University, reports that more than 90 percent of negotiators fail to ask "diagnostic questions" that relate to preferences, values, goals, fears, and so on. If the questions were answered, her research shows, the negotiations would be significantly improved. Beyond data, the questions that reveal stories are incredibly helpful in framing negotiations, and we'll circle back to the power of stories in later chapters.

What I appreciated so much about Doc and Clark was how methodical and emotion-free both were about Setting the Stage. It's so important to look ahead and ask, "What if I get what I want?" Gathering as much data on the front end helps position the negotiation for greater success and builds all-important confidence going into making the ask.

ACTIONS ARE GREATER THAN WORDS

As you collect data, one of the most important aspects is to study the other side as it is studying you. Hundreds of negotiations have taught me the same basic needs that both sides have and reinforced the idea that we are constantly observing the other side for evidence that will help us come to a conclusion. Observing actions is more powerful than listening. In fact, you should assume that the other side isn't even listening to you. Those needs can be summed up with these questions:

- Do I like you?

- Can you help me?

- Do I trust you?

This is a great way to segue into the next tool: Finding Common Ground. These questions will follow you as you move forward in successful negotiations.

SUMMARY

Being prepared is more than half the work of negotiating. You have to be able to research the data and understand what they represent in the abstract. Setting the Stage means doing your homework before you enter a negotiation so that you know exactly where you stand. By doing so, you enter negotiations on a solid footing and set yourself up for success.

How do you Set the Stage?

- **Know the basic facts.** What do you want? What does the other side want? The answer isn't always written on paper. You need to know the intangibles in every deal.

- **Develop 360-Degree Awareness.** Know the goals, needs, gaps, values, and fears of the other side. These data will be even more valuable as your strategy unfolds throughout the negotiation.

- **Grasp your comparables.** Comps are a baseline for negotiating. Start with knowing what you are worth in the market and always factor in what is at stake besides money.

- **Know why.** The fears and desires of both sides will drive what each is willing to sacrifice in pursuit of a goal.

- **Determine the inner baseline.** Understanding the motivations of the other side as well as your own will open more choices, which will create more engagement and willingness in negotiation.

- **Deal with the right trigger person.** Who will be making the decision (who is the point person) for the other side? Who are the influencers? These are not always the people you think.

- **Don't make assumptions.** Ask the most thorough questions so that you can prevent gaps and blind spots. Doing this now will save you time (and regret) as the deal unfolds.

- **Actions are greater than words.** Study the other side. In the early stages of negotiation, both sides want to know three simple things: Do I like you? Can you help me? Do I trust you? If and how these questions are answered early can set the tone for success.

Finding Common Ground

Fear. It's the reason most people do not like to negotiate. Fear comes from seeing the gap between where they are and where they want to be. It's like looking across a canyon to a beautiful resort. All you can see is the drop-off and no way to get to the resort.

But there is a way to get across that gap. It's finding a bridge, a common ground between you and the other side that allows you both to cross. To Find Common Ground, you have to take a hard look at your data—your comps, market research, and everything else you have gathered to Set the Stage—and move into the creative side of your brain.

FINDING THE WAY HOME

At age 24 I was living in Atlanta, trying to make it as a sports agent with barely any clients. To say that money was tight was an understatement. My lack of resources was a big hindrance to my goal of seeing my parents in Lansing, 775 miles north. That was a big canyon.

I could save for a plane ticket but didn't want to have to wait that long. Was there any chance my employer would fly me up there? I started to think about how that would look, to see what common ground I could establish between me and a business deal that would persuade my employer to send me to Michigan.

The Detroit Tigers were an obvious target. We were starting to represent more baseball players, but who in the big leagues would talk to a no-name like me? I knew none of them personally, and there are no cold calls in professional sports—none that work, anyway. The circles around these athletes are too tight. It's human nature to respond to a gift rather than a request, so I had to find something I could offer them that would get their attention.

Once I had that, I had to find someone who was already sharing common ground with them and see if that person would trust me enough to make an introduction.

I didn't know a ton of people at that point, but some guys I did know ran a water company. They wanted to get into major league clubhouses. All kinds of companies ship free merchandise to club-houses in the hope that the players will be interested in the free products and give them an entrée into a business relationship. Getting its product tied to a successful athlete is a major coup for a business because pro athletes have such powerful platforms; fans see them as role models and pay attention to the brands they advertise.

I asked the water guys if they would consider shipping a case of their water to the Tigers' clubhouse as a gift to 25 guys who might be a little thirsty from playing baseball. Maybe this could evolve into their product becoming the official water of the Detroit Tigers. They could care less about my getting to see my parents, but they were very interested in me helping open the door to Tiger Stadium for them.

Now I just had to find a gatekeeper who would help me (and the free water) get into the clubhouse.

I knew a wealth manager for some of the Tigers and reached out to him.

"Who's the nicest guy on the Tigers, with the most potential?" I asked my friend.

"Wow, I had never thought about it quite that way before," my friend replied, and paused. "Mike Maroth, by far. Mike Maroth."

Mike Maroth was a pitcher for the Tigers who had studied business administration at the University of Central Florida.

At that point, I had enough to go on to contact Maroth to see if I could talk to him about a possible endorsement with a water company. If he said yes (and ultimately he did), I planned to book the flight, see my parents, have lunch with Mike and his wife, Brooke, and give them information about our firm as well.

"We love our agent," Brooke said flat out at our lunch. Getting my foot in the door, I could tell, threatened the delicate relationship between the Maroths and their agent. I didn't want to push that, especially because I was trying to breathe some air into our own brand-new friendship.

"I'm glad to hear that," I replied. "No worries. I love to hear that a player's happy."

Then I immediately launched into the water deal.

Another bit of research I had done helped me move the conversation further to expand our common ground. I had a little bridge to him with the water; now could I shore that up?

I knew the Maroths held strong Christian beliefs, so I asked them about their charity work in Detroit.

"So many kids are hungry," Mike said. "And it's crazy how much food we have in the clubhouse that just goes to waste."

"Maybe that food could go to a shelter," I suggested. "I don't mind making a few calls."

From there we found a shelter that would pick up the clubhouse food after every home game, which made Mike happy; even more important, it made Brooke happy, too. The Maroths ended up

baseball careers, and helping them solve those challenges taught me important lessons about Finding Common Ground.

Mahay represents the importance of flexibility in this stage of negotiations. The more you can adapt to add value sought by the other side, the greater your power in negotiation will be.

Mahay had made it to the majors as an outfielder with the Boston Red Sox. He chose to be a replacement player during the 1994–1995 strike season. Afterward, he returned to the minors, where many careers end with little ceremony. But Mahay tried something different. He wasn't afraid of change or taking risks. Instead of being the guy waiting for a long ball to catch, he decided to become a pitcher. He was a lefthander, which made him more desirable to teams, but to perfect his transition, he had to drop deeper into the farm system, even spending time with a team in Australia. He finally got picked by the Oakland A's and played for nearly a dozen more teams before retiring in 2013.

Mahay kept his major league career going through creativity and risk taking. His move to pitching made him more attractive to teams and proved his versatility. With Mahay, they were getting two players for the price of one, and that increased the common ground between them.

Moehler was a right-handed pitcher who made his major league debut in 1996. A decade later, he needed about two months in the big leagues to qualify for his full pension. He was 50 days short of 10 years of service time, a threshold that would make him eligible for $100,000 a year for the rest of his life. Thus, we weren't just negotiating for two months of work; at stake was a chunk of his future income. Moehler was no Rudy, a kid who gets put in the end of the big game because he has a big heart. Moehler still had a good arm; in fact, he would put in several more solid years as a reliever until retiring from the Houston Astros in 2010. "He's a solid pitcher whose value doesn't always show up in the numbers. He keeps you in games and gives you a chance to win," Astros general manager Ed Wade said later to the press. "And, because of his makeup and work ethic, he's a great example for our young pitchers."

At that earlier juncture in his career, we were open and honest with potential teams, establishing the common ground of giving Moehler this chance to push across an incredibly important finishing line for major league veterans. To the Florida Marlins, Moehler's story probably wasn't as important as his status as a right-handed starter. When he signed with them and made his 10 years, I realized that when the deal is about something bigger than money—in this case long-term security—I feel the most rewarded. Doing right for people who deserve it is my biggest bonus.

FAVOR COLUMN

The end of Chapter 1 listed three questions that the other side—on some level, not always out loud—will be asking during a negotiation:

- Do I like you?
- Can you help me?
- Do I trust you?

These questions will follow you as you move forward in successful negotiations. One of the most powerful ways of answering these questions is by establishing a Favor Column.

Favor Columns represent the philosophy I live by as an agent. It is a strategy that has worked hundreds of times for me in negotiating with some of the toughest people to get in front of: professional athletes, coaches, and CEOs. Favor Columns enabled me to build relationships with people who are tough to get to and tough to connect with, who don't trust, and who question others' motives.

By building authenticity and trust with these tough clients, Favor Columns empowered me to be a deal maker and not a deal breaker. Favor Columns are a natural outgrowth of 360-Degree Awareness. You can build favor because you are fully aware of their world. You can surprise them with value because of your full-circle awareness. You can have one without the other, but together they produce the optimum results in negotiation—arguably for both sides.

A Favor Column is a series of actions that at first may be surprising to the other side in the negotiation but that in time they come to expect, and one day they wake up and realize they can't live without. Tactically, you are starting to work for the other side before having its business. Already you are respectfully finding ways to add value, contribute, and solve problems for them.

The Favor Column operates on the premise that people like people who help them, who improve their lives, who add value and enhance their lives. If people like you, they want to be around you and want to be associated with you. They want your help. You have introduced benefits into the conversation before you ask.

The Favor Column is powerful because people do not want to give up something that or someone who brings them efficiency, ease, and even happiness. They want to preserve the flow of favors. When you make the ask, they want to say yes.

If you think about your checkbook, you have columns for deposits and columns for withdrawals. Those columns work together to tell you how much you have in the bank. Relationships have a balance, too. You don't usually track them on paper, although a Favor Column represents a powerful way of doing just that. Favors are what you give to another person that makes him or her feel enriched.

I speak often and talk about Favor Columns with businesspeople. I understand that many industries, including the sports agent business, have rules and regulations about what can and can't be provided from a value perspective. For example, what might fall in a Favor Column includes an article that you believe would benefit the other person, an inexpensive book you know he or she would enjoy, a video you can e-mail that he or she would find interesting, and a framed picture of the two of you playing golf. The intent is to demonstrate to the other party, through your behavior and without being asked, that you care, that you are thinking about that person, and that you sincerely want to make his or her world better. What would your mom prefer? A framed picture of her grandchildren, a letter from you about how much you appreciate her, or a hundred dollar bill? Often it's the item that demonstrates more thought. It's the same with the Favor Column. You can build Favor Columns in ethical, inexpensive ways. Be creative.

Here's a recent favor that exemplifies my style of building a Favor Column. The Michigan State basketball team signed me up as a sponsor for its benefit golf tournament, which raises money for the athletic department; through my negotiations for Tom Izzo, I consider the team a stakeholder in my client's success, so I want to build favor with it.

I couldn't be in Lansing for the event, so my parents played in my sponsor foursome. You already know how close I am to them and how much fun I have making them happy. At the tournament, they were the oldest participants, and my dad, who plays golf weekly and has been a huge Spartan fan his whole life, got a big thrill from being on the same course with some of the university's top names.

After the tournament, I got an e-mail with a picture of my dad next to a golf hole and the subject line "Dad's first hole in one." Even before I called my dad, the thrill was palpable. This was a huge rush for me, too. What I thought was me doing a favor turned into the athletic department helping provide the stage for my dad to have an extraordinary (and extraordinarily lucky) memory.

I immediately texted the head coach, highlighting the platform she provided for my dad. "Our donation just doubled," I said. "You made it possible for my dad to get his first ever hole in one, at 76 years old." The money, warmth, and family memory helped me create a greater bond with my client's stakeholder. This is exactly what I want my Favor Columns to achieve.

The Favor Column is built on one word: *give*.

Give, give, give. Give with substance to add value to the person you wish to engage with, and all the while share your energy and your value.

Say someone takes home a car to see how it drives and feels. He or she sees how it looks in the driveway and garage. The car dealer is totally fine with this loan. The customer who gets used to the car, to the pleasure and comfort it gives him or her every day, is going to buy the car. And the dealer is operating on the Favor Column: investing in the relationship and giving trust, knowing that the loan builds relationships and ultimately a successful financial transaction.

It is critical to believe in the importance of giving to the other side in a negotiation. Essentially, you are modeling the behavior that you want from the other side. It may seem counterintuitive to give to the other side, but this is the way you bring to life the essence of what a relationship with you looks like—and feels like. You are sharing information that builds trust and shows understanding of the other side. The Favor Column can represent the foundation of a mutual win in negotiation.

MAKING TIME

You may be thinking, Molly, my negotiations turn on a dime. Nobody has time for Favor Columns.

What I'm saying is that everyone can absorb and adopt this mentality and find short, quick ways to build favors.

As a frequent flier with Delta Airlines, I receive snack and drink tickets that I can use when I fly coach, where drinks and snacks carry a price. I usually have four to six of these tickets in my purse. I think of them not as tickets but as Delta's contribution to my Favor Column. They work like cash for something I value a lot more than drinks or snacks: better seats when my family flies.

With five of us, sometimes we're lucky just to get that number of seats together on a popular flight, and so I have to go into negotiation mode in the tight space, literally, of a packed plane. I might be successful just asking nicely for someone to move so that we can sit together, but the guy in 32C is a heck of a lot more likely to say yes if I pull out a free snack coupon and offer him another aisle seat. As I extend my hand to him, I have little doubt that he will say, "Sure, no problem." The Favor Column is a win-win. It's the sweetener. Thanks, Delta!

Perhaps even more important than making the gesture is adopting this mode of relaxed, confident thinking: *How can I give to the person authentically while adding value to his or her world? And maybe, just maybe, some goodness will come back my way, but if not, no worries.*

I also argue that you can't afford to ignore Favor Columns. Although negotiations typically involve companies that employ skilled negotiators—you may fall into this category—more people are becoming their own employers. A study by the U.S. Commerce Department's Bureau of Economic Analysis showed that almost all the job growth in the United States from 2000 to 2011 was in self-employment; more than one in five workers are self-employed, and that number is rising. This means you are more likely to negotiate on your own behalf. The stakes are getting higher, and so is the value of a strong Favor Column. In business development—which is a long-term process, not a quick turnaround—the Favor Column becomes an even more critical tool.

Another important point: Finding Common Ground means establishing as strong a relationship as possible before making the ask. As you read this, you may be realizing that your difficulty negotiating is rooted in less than optimum relationships. Asking is so much easier and Asking with Confidence comes so much more naturally when you have built a great relationship with the other side over time.

COMMON GROUND WITHOUT A DEADLINE

It's very tough to build a Favor Column with a deadline looming and a lot at stake. Even if you are facing that kind of a negotiation, keep the Favor Column in mind. There are probably other relationships in your world that will benefit tremendously if you begin to nurture them away from the negotiating process. These are the five steps to Favor Columns.

First, *Favor Columns are built from the heart, from a professional and respectful point of view.* This tool is built through genuine friendliness and the sincere belief that our services can be of help to the other person. I established the Maroth deal out of the sincere belief that I could help him, help the water company, and help myself get to see my parents. The belief part is key because I had to find the confidence and expectation that I would make contact with someone in the Tigers' clubhouse and that I believed in my value to make that athlete's life better.

Second, when you get that access and opportunity, *listen for clues.* What are the frustrations? Concerns? Questions? Desires? Fears? Where are the needs that are not being met? Ask simple questions if necessary but don't interrogate. This shouldn't be complicated for you or the other side.

Third, *observe*. This is where I gained a foothold into Maroth's world. I got clear on his values and what wasn't being met in his life and then got busy with favors (such as organizing the multiple sclerosis events) that would blow him away while doing good.

Fourth, make a list of *what that person needs and wants.* The list is based on the clarity gained in the first three steps. Make this list as long as possible. Put yourself in that person's shoes. What would make that person feel good? Her life easier? Her problems solved?

Five, *consider timing.* A Favor Column doesn't work like a random delivery of a gift basket or floral arrangement. It's more targeted. For example, if I know an athlete's favorite band is coming to town for a concert, I'll snap up tickets and have them delivered before he even thinks about clearing his calendar. A Favor Column is about service, and great service leads to very favorable negotiations.

FAVOR COLUMNS CREATE COMMON GROUND

The Favor Column is a way to set up a successful negotiation and ongoing relationship with the other side. Most of us are in a competitive field, and our negotiations take place in that context. We have to prove ourselves against others who provide similar goods or services. One of the most common—and most difficult—negotiations is to sign a new client. The Favor Column is the preview of coming attractions for a client. These gestures show what you can do, how you think, and how you execute. It shows that you are proactive and insightful and can take action before being asked. A Favor Column gives them a sense of your style, approach, timing, and sense of urgency around their business. It's an unofficial test period. In our supercompetitive world, people want the attention that a Favor Column represents.

A Favor Column sets you up as different from your competition. My goal was for a potential client to think, "My agent doesn't do all that Molly does for me—and Molly doesn't even have my business! I better hire Molly. If I don't, I'm going to be stuck with Average Agent, and how can I live without all these favors?" Favors delivered in an honest, open, reliable manner build a deep level of trust. The recipient learns that he or she can count on you to come through.

Successful creation of a Favor Column will create the answers to the three questions we have been discussing:

- Do I like you? *You bet!*
- Can you help me? *Yes, you've proved it.*
- Do I trust you? *Implicitly.*

The Favor Column sets up the ask. Without the Favor Column, you are really no different from anyone else who wants someone's business. Without that foundation, you must sell through words only. With a track record of favors, you have demonstrated that actions speak louder than words.

WITH DISCONNECTS, USE CURIOSITY

All this may sound easy, as if it were just a matter of mindset. The higher the stakes and the harder the deadline, the more difficult it is to establish common ground. The Favor Column is an offensive tool, but you also need a good defense.

How do you deal with the other side when it pushes back or is even hostile early in negotiations? What if it rejects favors or you see no opportunity for that tool? What if the response is negative? Withholding information is the tool of intimidation, so where do you go at that point?

Human nature makes us dig in our own heels, but that's almost always counterproductive at this stage of the negotiations. The best way to deal with this kind of pushback is counterintuitive. You may have to dig up inner reserves you didn't know you had, but I promise you that if you do, it will be well worth it. *Instead of getting defensive, become curious.*

That's right. When the other side rejects your efforts to establish common ground, remain open. Put your feelings aside and go into fact-collecting mode. Rejection and hostility are open doors if you see them that way. Curiosity is an important tool for moving away from personalities and understanding the problem. It gives you a way forward without arguing and confrontation, which you want to avoid if at all possible.

Guaranteed, there are going to be disconnects during negotiations; that's why so few people enjoy trying to work through conflict to get to agreement. My goal when faced with a disconnect is to attempt to become curious about the other side's perspective. This has the added benefit of giving the other side a chance to feel heard. It is an incredibly powerful tool for closing the gap.

If you are arguing even before making the ask, that's setting an atmosphere of animosity and antagonism that will never go away. When the other side begins with hostility, curiosity can give you a way to pursue forward movement and create confidence and trust. Curiosity takes courage: the courage to ask questions that are difficult. It is a gutsy means of closing the gap with the other side because it shows how serious you are about hearing what it has to say.

Before I get further into the power of curiosity, let me emphasize how challenging and necessary this is. For various reasons—cultural, personality, maybe even physiological factors such as hormones—many people feel that they cannot get past their own feelings. It may be an entrenched sense of being right (some call this entitlement). I'm no psychologist, but I can attest to the damage that this mentality inflicts on negotiation. *You must develop empathy to be an effective negotiator.*

Negotiation depends on closing the distance between two sides, not increasing it. When your feelings take over the conversation, a successful negotiation becomes further out of reach. You are going to lose ground when buying your dream house if the agent knows how much you adore it; the same is true for a car. Great emotion reduces the ability to recover when a negotiation fails; the more personal you make a negotiation, the harder it is to reposition yourself if and when the dialogue with the other side breaks down.

FINDING THE WRONG COMMON GROUND: BILLY DONOVAN

Let me share a story that shows the importance of Finding Common Ground, because sometimes what you think is common ground is really an illusion.

I mentioned Billy Donovan in the Introduction; he's the University of Florida coach whom we hooked up with the Orlando Magic only to have him back off the deal. No one was hotter than Donovan in college basketball in 2007. By winning back-to-back national championships, he was among only seven coaches who could say that and the first in 15 years. He was among only two people in NCAA Division I history who have played in a Final Four, served as an assistant coach in a Final Four, and participated in a Final Four as a head coach. He would eventually become the youngest winner of the Wooden Award as a Legend of Coaching. He brought in more fans to Florida and turned out more NBA draft picks than almost anyone else. By representing Donovan at the top of his game, we were assumed to be at the top of ours.

Why did this deal fall apart? We discovered we had misread two key relationships: the one between him and us and the one between him and the Florida athletic director. This breakdown led to great insight into the power of relationships and taking the important risk early in negotiation of identifying and testing those relationships.

We thought we were clear on what Donovan wanted after winning back-to-back national championships: a job in the pros in the same state where many basketball fans already knew and loved him as a winner. He would have greater visibility and make more money; if he won in the pros, all that would expand because the stage is so much greater than in college hoops. What we didn't do so well was lay out how this new ground in the NBA was going to negate the old ground he knew so well at Florida. By signing with the Magic, Donovan would have to thank his old boss, fans, and players and probably leave the insular town of Gainesville with folks feeling betrayed.

This is what we are used to seeing, and we thought Donovan knew what he was in for. At his press conference announcing his exit from Florida, he was poised and assured while issuing the kind of news that turns the college basketball world on its head. Florida would go after the best replacement in the country, setting off a ripple of replacements across the sport. Donovan wasn't breaking a sweat. After he finished signing his multiple contracts with the Magic and we got into the limo, I remember thinking, This guy is tough as nails.

The next morning he called. He had spent the night reflecting on his decision and realizing he had made a mistake. "I don't want the NBA job. Never mind. I'll stay at Florida." Flabbergasted doesn't begin to cover the feeling. There are a few unprintable descriptions, as you might imagine, but Donovan was clear. He had changed his mind, and it was our job to unwind the deal.

We had thought he was more than ready to give up the old ground he had shared with his boss, Jeremy Foley. We knew that there was loyalty there. Foley clearly believed in Donovan and demonstrated that belief. "Foley was once so befuddled that his program-builder won two national titles and zero conference coach of the year awards that he had a plaque made for Donovan," Yahoo! Sports reported, and then quoted Foley: "Sometimes [Donovan's] not accorded the respect he deserves."

In the heat of the transition to the pros, I believe Donovan at some point had a crisis of conscience and doubted if anyone at the Magic—maybe in the NBA—would be as good as Foley was at having his back. We thought the deal was about Donovan's ambition—about money, status, a new challenge, and a new platform—but that relationship with Foley was his anchor. Even after he signed with the Magic, it pulled him back to Gainesville. My gut feeling is that he looked back at all the great Florida fans and Foley, who is a great athletic director, and doubted himself. What am I doing? is a question that can sabotage any negotiation.

This story points out that no deals happen in a vacuum. It's not rocket science to realize that you need to establish common ground in a negotiation. It's much more difficult to identify *the most solid common ground*. What is most at stake for each side? What are the buttons that will be pushed? Yes, Donovan was clear with us, but was he *really, really* clear? Just like an engineer who watches a building or bridge fall down, a negotiator learns to take a belt and suspenders approach to establishing common ground. It's a hard way to learn that it's not enough to Find Common Ground; you've got to inspect each square inch.

This is all incredibly important groundwork for a successful negotiation and is shown in relief by deals like Donovan's that blow up. We had every reason to feel defensive. Where did we go wrong? We honestly asked that question, turning our defensiveness into curiosity. We wanted to learn as much as possible about our client and ourselves through this breakdown, to salvage what we could from our embarrassment. Was this easy? Not at all, because it went against our human nature. Deciding to be curious instead of defensive reflects the *strategic understanding of emotion in negotiation*. It is important not to take anything personally in a negotiation, even when you are negotiating for yourself.

This episode made me and my firm make an even more concerted effort to look holistically at each client, to study clients as dynamic individuals, and to ask hard questions separate from our own financial interests. We learned to dig even deeper to get the content that would provide an authentic foundation for a successful deal. You can bet that we broke down the domino effect for every subsequent client to make sure he or she understood the ramifications of the deal.

"Let's play this out. Imagine twenty-four months from now if your pro job doesn't work out," I'm likely to say now. "You're a young guy. You could go back to the college game, to a program that's somewhere in the middle and maybe in the middle of nowhere. How are you going to feel coming back to college level?"

My common ground with my client became based on an even fuller disclosure on the front end. Finding Common Ground includes the decision to play devil's advocate and peel back the image clients may have about the greener pastures. In Donovan's case, the NBA was not the utopia that many top college coaches believe it will be.

Donovan ultimately made me a better negotiator; I had more motivation to go deeper with my clients and take more risks, which led to more trust between us. This is also counterintuitive. We are more likely to avoid introducing other factors into the negotiation for fear that they will sabotage success. I have come to believe that this grounded, reality-check conversation— where I lay out all the common mistakes that I have seen and can see—is part of creating a 360-Degree Awareness in my client so that he or she can make the best decision, regardless of financial repercussions.

Here are some questions that are worth asking about common ground:

1. What are the other side's goals and options?
2. What's its preferred option? What part of this option is easiest for me to offer?
3. What's its second option?
4. Can I make my deal at least better than the second option?
5. Can I make any of the competing options less attractive?
6. What am I willing to sacrifice to make this deal?
7. What am I not willing to sacrifice?

I lay this out for professional golfers who are lured by the big deals offered if they switch equipment. Their success hinges on the slightest edges of confidence and skill, and they must have implicit trust in the clubs and balls they choose. Establishing common ground with them means helping them dig down deep and understand what a change looks like. How much extra time will they be spending practicing in November and December to make sure they feel great about their new equipment? Switching is great only if you can still do what you do best and maybe do it even better; this is the risk that goes with a deal like this. And yes, these conversations can cause the deal to implode.

Another example of this conversation is with a team athlete such as a baseball player who is considering an offer from another team. It's not just about the money; players are representing a community, and in that place there are relationships in which they are invested. An agent can negotiate for a salary contract and shove it through, but if I am going to maintain my relationships with that athlete, I need to preview as best as I can the possible ways in which important relationships are going to change. An athlete usually has experienced new teammates, but there are often key people and sponsors who will be shaken when that athlete makes a major move, and the athlete often hasn't learned to take these kinds of relationships into consideration. For the athlete, this conversation is necessary for building 360-Degree Awareness. For me, it's about identifying potential Jeremy Foleys—the anchors that may be so important to a client that a negotiation can fall apart.

BEHIND EACH PERSON IS A TEAM

In September 2013, 64-year-old Diana Nyad became the first person to swim from Cuba to Florida without a shark cage. The 110-mile journey took her nearly 53 hours to complete and was her fifth attempt at achieving her lifelong dream.

As Nyad swam to shore, severely dehydrated, sunburned, disoriented, and exhausted, she shared this: "I have three messages. One is, we should never, ever give up. Two is, you're never too old to chase your dream. Three is, it looks like a solitary sport, but it is a team."

Wow, I thought to myself as I watched the news coverage. After 53 solitary hours in the water, what a time to talk about the team. She relied on mental tricks such as counting her strokes in different languages and scrolling through her playlist of 85 songs. It seemed like an incredible individual feat.

But Nyad was swift to talk about how she had relied on a 35-person support team of high-tech experts to achieve her goal. The team included doctors who watched her health and navigators who kept her on course. The team had equipment that generated a faint electrical field that was designed to keep sharks at bay. Five boats of team members were "working like a machine" throughout her swim, she said. Divers continuously circled her to watch for sharks, and kayakers surrounded her to create a protective barrier as best they could. She even had a jellyfish expert in the water who would scoop up sea creatures that might have stung her. The support crew monitored her health and wellness 24/7 throughout the swim, providing nutrition when possible and guiding her the entire 110 miles.

In a negotiation, you don't want to be like me watching Nyad come out of the water, astounded at all the stakeholders in her success. You want to know that even the most solitary achievement is not possible without a team and that the people behind the people you are negotiating with can have a huge influence on how your negotiation goes.

Pay attention to who the other side references, who it answers to and looks up to. The benefits of a successful negotiation will ripple through its world, and you will want to know if and how these potential beneficiaries are exerting influence. By finding out the depth and interests of the entire team represented in the negotiation, you will have the greatest chance of Finding Common Ground.

BOBBY COX AND A BAG FULL OF PAYCHECKS

Bobby Cox is one of the greatest baseball managers of all time, and I count it among my greatest honors to have represented him in various negotiations. He was passionate about being paid fairly in this ultracompetitive field, and I felt relieved and happy when we were able to negotiate deals that satisfied him.

Imagine my surprise when our controller called and told me he wasn't cashing his checks and they needed to get that cash off the books.

Bobby had been keeping the checks in his team bag and was in no hurry to deposit them. As important as it had been that he be paid fairly, he was just as cavalier about blowing off the actual money. That taught me that what is truly important to people like Bobby Cox is what the money represents: *respect*. Learning from observing his behavior after the negotiation helped me understand how best to Find Common Ground for his next negotiations, to know what was most important to him even when he did not express it in words.

Actions are more important in terms of understanding a person's values, and these actions are on display before, during, and after a negotiation. Just as Bobby's expectation of his players was based on their prior performance, my expectation of behavior by either side is rooted in past negotiations. Finding Common Ground is done best when you have clarity on what is most important to both sides, and it's important to stay alert for any behaviors that provide clues to what each side needs, wants, and fears. Remember that most of the most important communication is nonverbal.

My long-term success hinges on the client feeling so solid about what he or she wants and needs that we are partners in the deal and go forward together as a team to succeed. Yes, this philosophy of pursuing 360-Degree Awareness does cost me some deals, but in the long run it has built me trust among people whose trust is rarely secured. They view my questions as a safeguard and a demonstration that I have their best interests foremost in my mind.

Asking questions is a great way of Finding Common Ground. So is tightening the circle of people who are knowledgeable about the negotiations. In high-profile deals, I have always found it best to stay out of negotiating in the media, because doing so creates and maintains trust. I try to keep communication as clear and simple as possible so that the other side knows that I am serious and stable about the common ground that I have offered in our negotiation.

Thus, although the Donovan story reads like a failure and sure felt like it at the time, I gained an invaluable understanding from it. No matter what happens in a negotiation, you want to first do no harm. No one should end up in an unhealthy place as a result of your efforts. The goal is to alleviate stress by Finding Common Ground. Getting there requires transparency, and sometimes that alone may cost you some deals. In the long run, the due diligence of finding clarity at this stage of the negotiation is worth it. No negotiation happens in a vacuum, and the way you handle yourself at every stage of a deal shapes your reputation and your ability to handle the next one.

Fortunately, our relationship with the Magic, from the owners to the GM, was such that they knew our intent was authentic in both securing and rewinding the deal. Our history with them had built a healthy foundation that made the rewinding process efficient and productive. Billy appreciated our understanding and willingness to walk on coals immediately upon his change of heart. Jeremy Foley, the athletic director at Florida, was able to look past a *big* hiccup and embrace our reboot. All of this—all of it—without exception was due to healthy and transparent relationships. That is also the reason the relationships still exist. Whether in a productive or a challenging spot in a negotiation, Finding Common Ground will benefit all parties.

SUMMARY

One primary reason people do not like to negotiate is fear—fear of confronting the gap between where they are and where they want to be. To bridge that gap, you must Find Common Ground between you and the other side. Long-term success hinges on the other side feeling that you are partners in the deal and that a mutual solution is possible.

Finding Common Ground relies on these practices:

- **Develop trust.** Consistently fulfilling expectations creates a safe zone where relationships flourish and both sides understand that their needs will be met.

- **Maintain flexibility.** The more you can adapt to and add value sought by the other side, the greater your power in negotiation is.

- **Build Favor Columns.** It may seem counterintuitive, but adding value demonstrates what a relationship with you is like. Giving with substance enables you to build relationships with people who are otherwise difficult to connect with. Favor Columns are the answer to the simple question: How can I give to a person—authentically—so that that person might give back to me?

- **Invest time and intention.** Establish as strong a relationship as possible before making the ask. When you have taken the time to build a great relationship, it's easier to Ask with Confidence.

- **Counter disconnects with curiosity.** When the other side expresses resistance or hostility, respond with curiosity and openness—never defensiveness. Curiosity is a tool for moving away from personalities and toward understanding the problem.

- **Be wary of great emotion.** Great emotion reduces the ability to recover when a negotiation fails. The more personal you make a negotiation, the harder it is to reposition.

- **Pay attention to context.** No negotiation happens in a vacuum. The way you handle yourself at every stage of negotiation forms your reputation and your ability to handle the next one. Push for common ground early and clearly.

Asking with Confidence

You know by now that I'm close with my folks, who modeled for me some of the fearless, insightful behavior that influenced my success as a negotiator. One purchase that my mom spurred me to negotiate illustrates the importance of Asking with Confidence and the elements of doing that.

Callaway Gardens is a lovely resort just south of Atlanta that's perfect for a family getaway. Mom and I were in some antique stores when she saw a piece of art and a flower arrangement that she loved.

"Molly, I really want both of those, but it's nine hundred bucks," she said to me. "I don't want to spend that kind of money. Maybe five hundred, but not nine hundred."

I went over to take a look. The picture didn't do a lot for me personally, but I'd do anything to make my mom happy. Getting the two items for about half price wouldn't be easy; I'd have to frame a good bit of positive emotion around this ask.

To do that, I needed her to step back. Her emotion and appearance might get in the way of negotiating on her behalf, just as they would if she were a major league baseball player in arbitration, so I politely told her it would be a lot easier if she wasn't around.

After she left, I approached the older guys in charge of the store.

"Hey, you know that picture of the guy who looks like he's from *Shaft*?" I said.

They nodded.

"And there's a flower arrangement; my mom loves that, too," I said.

Yes, they knew what I was talking about. I could tell right away that these guys were pretty straight up.

"Is nine hundred your best price on those together?"

They look at each other. One guy is definitely going to do the talking.

"I could do seven seventy-five," he says. I can tell he wants to deal.

"Look, my mom can't do six hundred for that print," I say, avoiding any sort of crazy excitement but expressing a polite interest in their goods. I want them to be part of our family story and buy into it. There's a touch of enthusiasm in my voice as well.

"And she and my dad would love to have that and the flower arrangement as a way to remember this special weekend that our family had together."

They're nodding and being understanding because they had seen us together in the store. (If Mom had stayed, they might have looked her over more carefully for signs that she had the means to pay full price. Another good reason for her to be absent.)

"What if we get both for four fifty?" I ask without a trace of doubt in my voice.

One guy looks at me, then at the other guy.

"Oh, man, shoot," he says, and I can tell he's doing the math in his head.

"Well, I got five hundred in this print and then I got the flowers," he says. "I can do seven hundred."

I keep working him.

"C'mon, man," I say with a smile. My tone is relaxed and friendly. I was confident and firm, projecting the knowledge that there was nothing about me not to like.

I could tell they wanted to say yes to me and be part of my enthusiasm for their merchandise and, even more important, part of the story of making my mom superhappy.

This isn't second nature, not after all these years; it's my nature, period. This moment of the ask is where I feel most at home, and it's why my family—my first home team—still turns to me to get the suites and cottages and other arrangements for our vacations together. It's why my kids' orthodontist agreed to a significant discount for cash up front for braces for all three of them.

At the antique store there's a pause.

"How about four ninety-five?" I say.

He nods. By the end of the transaction, he had bubble wrapped and delivered the purchases to our bed-and-breakfast for safe transport back to Michigan.

The next day, we were back in Atlanta for the Final Four, the stage for the top teams in college basketball. So much of what I know to be true about negotiating is reflected in the great performances I have witnessed on the court or the field.

For instance, time and time again I have seen great sporting events turn on a swift, timely action by an athlete. It might be the perfect throw to get a runner out at home or the jump shot at the end of the game that wins the contest. These actions cannot be scripted, and they depend on great confidence; the athlete believes that he or she can perform in situations with the greatest pressure. Not only can the athlete perform, but he or she wants the ball in that situation, wants to take the risk of winning or failing.

That confident leadership may be inborn for some gifted athletes; I believe that we can acquire greater confidence by emulating those great performers. We do that through two main avenues: precision and practice. Just as a great athlete is decisive at the right time, a confident ask is precise and time-sensitive. There's no waffling, no hemming and hawing. We're talking about an action taken at the right time that lasts just as long as it needs to and then ends without a sense of looking back or regret. Confidence, as great athletes will tell you, is based on selective memory.

Before I break down the elements of precision and practice, I want to explain why Asking with Confidence is so important.

THE PSYCHOLOGY OF THE ASK

We've talked about Setting the Stage and Finding Common Ground, which are the essential first two steps in a negotiation. You have learned why and how it's necessary to understand what the other side wants and fears and study its actions and ask questions to gain clarity on what is most at stake and identify the greatest influences and influencers. You understand the power of building a Favor Column, especially over time, and taking the risks that will establish long-term trust.

If you are laying this kind of groundwork well—achieving 360-Degree Awareness for yourself and, if you represent a client, for that person as well—you are telegraphing to the other side that you know what you are doing. You are sending consistent signals that establish your trustworthiness. Through transparent behavior, you have created expectancy. Your attentiveness points to an ask; the other side is primed and waiting for it.

AT THE ORTHODONTIST

My three daughters—twins and a sister born within a year of each other—have the kind of teeth that look like a land mine went off in each mouth: teeth everywhere they shouldn't be. In my area, braces go for $3,000 a kid. I got to know the orthodontist, and her business operates like those of many entrepreneurs. She bills clients as the work is done, and enough clients pay in time for her to clear a profit. It's important to study anxiety points like this. I saw what a pain it was for her office to track the records of every single kid and family and payer. That was a burden I was ready to relieve when we sat down to discuss our orthodontia game plan.

You might be thinking that no one negotiates with medical professionals such as orthodontists, but to me, most everything is negotiable. The orthodontist may not negotiate many deals like the one I was going to propose, but she's already had to negotiate with insurance companies, suppliers, and who knows who else. All businesses do; the challenge is to draw a person into negotiating in an area that may be nontraditional.

She goes over what my girls need and quotes me $3,000 for each girl's orthodontic work.

"What if I give you six K up front for all three?" I counter. "It'll be simpler for you to be paid in advance and not have to mess with any billing."

She doesn't think long. "Done," she says.

And it was. I wrote the check, and my girls are getting their teeth straightened.

Yes, this deal involved a good bit of trust from me that I wouldn't get shafted on service, or that this orthodontist wasn't going to leave town before the job was done. I bet against that on the basis of her reputation. She knows, too, that a great deal for me can result in intangible marketing benefits as I advertise her among my deep base of neighbors and clients who are connected through social media. Part of our deal involved her being able to take before and after photos of my daughters' teeth. I was able to Ask with Confidence because my trust was high. The higher the risk of the ask is, the more trust you need before you can Ask with Confidence. There has to be enough trust that you truly believe in what you are asking for enough to overcome any doubt that it is worth asking for. Confidence comes from a place of safety and trust.

ASKING IS HARD

The ask is the point in negotiating that makes people feel most uncomfortable and fearful. Forget confidence; we're talking about being afraid to ask *at all*. The main fear is that the other side will push back, say no, and close the door. Asking makes you vulnerable. We are saying that we need something, and we are naming it and putting it in its world.

The fear of asking is well documented. Salary.com interviewed nearly 2,000 people on this subject and noted, "Failure to argue your self-worth often means leaving thousands of dollars on the table, and can potentially cost you millions of dollars over the course of your life. Yet our research found nearly one-fifth of workers never negotiate after they're offered a job." The cost of not negotiating can be more than $500,000 by the time an employee is age 60, and more than three-quarters of the respondents said they regretted not negotiating for more money after being offered a job.

Why didn't they negotiate? The biggest reason was fear that they would lose their jobs. Other reasons included lack of negotiating skills and confidence and a dislike of negotiating. They didn't want to come across as greedy, didn't picture a way to try it, or didn't think it would make a difference. A lot of roadblocks to negotiating are cultural: we value independence and self-reliance, and asking always implies a shift in power and control.

Asking is a seed. It will either take root or wither, and the outcome depends on many factors beyond your control. Asking shifts control away from the person asking and feels as if you are giving all the choices to the other side. This is understandably frightening, especially to a person without experience, but as I will explain, it's not always true.

It's worth drilling down to the fear messages you may be hearing. Some people call this monkey chatter. When you can identify these detrimental messages, you can start replacing them with your greater truth. Find an alternative behavior that can become your new action. If you have trouble with making an ask, here are some mantras:

> The other side likes me and what I have offered so far.
>
> The other side knows I will help it.
>
> The other side has shown that it believes I am trustworthy.

This may sound corny. Of course you are going to need to put this in your own words. I put this out there because self-talk and visualization are the core habits of successful athletes and other high achievers, especially those who perform well in difficult circumstances. They have highly tuned defense mechanisms that shut out the negative voices; they listen to their own message of confidence and see themselves succeeding even before the ball touches their hands or the other side has heard their pitch. They embody what Henry David Thoreau said: "As a single footstep will not make a path on the earth, so a single thought will not make a pathway in the mind. To make a deep physical path, we walk again and again. To make a deep mental path, we must think over and over the kind of thoughts we wish to dominate our lives."

High achievers show that it is possible to ask even when part of us thinks we cannot, but only if our desire can gain an edge over our fear. Self-talk is a powerful way to change your reality; some psychologists think it may be the *only* way. Positive self-talk gives us a better chance to cope with threatening situations and leads to greater emotional resilience, which then sets us up for more positive results. Elite performers believe the best is going to happen, not the worst, and their internal script is filled with unspoken positive thoughts that help fulfill their vision of success.

According to the Mayo Clinic, positive thinking carries health benefits such as increased life span, lower rates of depression and distress, and fewer colds and reduced risk of death from heart disease. The benefit I like best is "better coping skills during hardship and times of stress." What that says to me is that anyone who uses positive self-talk is going to cope better with negotiating and have a greater chance of success. Positive self-talk is a script that can talk down the fear that keeps you from Asking with Confidence.

BUILDING CONFIDENCE

In sports and other industries, there is a certain mindset that skills are born within us and cannot be learned. Confidence is certainly a trait that seems to come naturally to people who go into negotiating and one that perpetuates itself. You feel confident, and you are successful; that makes you feel confident, and so on. If confidence is part of a chicken-and-egg question, do you have to have it to begin with? How do you get it?

This is where precision and practice form a powerful tag team that builds confidence. You have already read about and I hope put into practice one example of precision + practice = confidence. When you turn defensiveness into curiosity, you exhibit a deft awareness at the right time. That's precision. If you've done it more than once, you have begun to practice this kind of precision. Over time, this habit is a powerful way to build confidence. Let's break it down further.

PRECISION

Just as a great athlete is decisive at the right time, a confident ask is precise and time-sensitive. The what, where, and how are specific and clear. Your ask involves a deadline or start time that beckons the other side to action. There's no throat clearing or backing away.

An ask can unfold in a series of moments, such as my example at the beginning of this chapter. I had a first ask ("What if we get both for four fifty?") and a follow-up ("How about four ninety-five?") within just a few minutes. Asking with precision may sound like plain common sense, but I've seen many negotiations break down because of a lack of attention to the basics.

Ask for What You Want

This sounds obvious, so I'll ask you to dig a little deeper. Asking for *what you want* is not the same as asking for *what you think you will get* or what the other side *won't mind giving you.* You cannot get a precise result if you don't know exactly what you want.

In my work as an agent, knowing what my client wants is the starting point for an ask. When that changes, so do the negotiations, and this is when it gets tricky. In Chapter 2, I mentioned Mike Maroth, the Detroit Tigers pitcher I ended up representing. As good an athlete as he was, with the kind of vision he had for striking out batters, he could not envision himself making more than about $100,000 a year.

When we negotiated for him, we asked the team to match the comps for a left-handed pitcher. The team lowballed Maroth, but we are duty-bound, much like real estate agents, to present even ridiculous offers to our client.

"This is so disrespectfully low, Mike," we told him. "You realize that the Major League Baseball Players Association will tell you that you shouldn't take this deal." The players association, which is a union, aims to bring salaries up. "We can lean on the team and get your bonuses structured, and you can make more."

"I'll take it," he said.

We were honest and transparent. We pointed out that he was affecting the market, that other left-handed pitchers would come in and face lower offers because he was accepting this one. It amazed us when he took the deal. In my mind, the other side was horrible, but we were honest the entire way, and these deals worked for him. What can you do? Particularly when you believe in transparency.

Maroth knew what he wanted. He was grateful for the platform of Major League Baseball. He was happy to make six figures. He wanted things to be fair, but he never wanted to push. It was okay for him to have a deal that would come over the ESPN crawl as a middle-of-the-road deal. Maroth may have wanted the process to be over because it made him nervous. When you have that mindset, you will walk away with less in hand than you would have if you had employed patience. Ultimately, what Maroth wanted and what we wanted for Maroth were two different things. We asked for what we wanted him to have, and he said yes to the deal that the other side gave him. We felt that this deal was well under market value and hurt other players by setting a precedent for a much lower comp.

That's tough for us, because we as agents see there is more room. In our business model, and as I believe is best and most ethical, the client has the final say on what he or she wants in the deal and what he or she will accept. The more competitive your field is (the more comps are in play), the more you will affect the market by not being clear on what you want. In this case, Maroth's acceptance was an outlier because most players would have rejected the offer. But the end result is the same: the left-handed pitchers who negotiated in Maroth's wake had to work around his lower comps.

The bottom line is that what you ask for forms a baseline for others who ask. That is the wide ripple effect of negotiating. Your target should be shaped by what you see happening after you are successful. Remember the story about the genie granting the wish? I think some people don't ask for what they want because they are on some level afraid of it. Fear is the number one enemy of successful negotiations, and asking for what you want and Asking with Confidence can happen with authenticity only when there is no fear. Fear and confidence cannot coexist.

To get clarity, sometimes I ask myself a simple two-part question: What would I be excited about if we got it, and excited about if we didn't? The answer helps me pinpoint my biggest reach. I don't ever want to have to give up too much to get the deal done, and these questions help me define that inflection point. It's a sweet spot. I'm competitive, too, and I have to separate that desire to win from the possibility that I may lose too much by doing so. I never want to lose my focus, my drive, and why I do this. Each time

I negotiate, I remind myself that I am starting over and must be as precise as possible in asking for what I want.

Importance of Choice

Precision doesn't mean narrowness. (Say that with me three times.) It's important to be precise and offer choice. Both of these elements combine to build an attractive ask and add to your authority.

Choice is important because it offers a sense of control and mutual benefit. Most parents know that they can get their kids to do something if they give them some sort of power of choice. This is as simple as, "You can clean up your toys now and I'll help you or you can clean them up later by yourself."

When there is only one choice, you're hurting your chances. You have presented only one door that the other side can walk through. There is either that one option or nothing. You have a 50–50 chance. You expand that a great deal when you offer more choices: "I can do X, Y, or Z, and this is what each scenario will mean or require." As we pointed out before, people don't negotiate because they fear losing control. Choice restores that sense of control. It also signals creativity and openness. "My way or the highway" is a mentality that allows little room for resourceful problem solving, which is often what negotiation boils down to.

One easy way to create choice is to take the other side's position and frame it as a question. Here's a hypothetical example from my antique store deal:

"I can do seven hundred," the guy says to me.

"So your best deal is seven hundred?" I say to him.

Turning his statement into a question gives him a choice to affirm or deny it. It also points out that the ask is often a series of questions to determine the exact position of the other side. A great negotiator can always keep asking questions to get clarity (and, as we'll talk about in Chapter 4, knows when to clam up).

I imagine each question, especially the ask ("What if we get both for four fifty?"), being like a medicine ball. You need to have strength, great reflexes, and flexibility to hold up this big heavy ball. People who do this kind of fitness training release all kinds of adrenaline. So does negotiating. It's like fencing or tennis, a back-and-forth that rewards strategy and perseverance. Keep asking, keep extracting, and don't take anything personally.

In the academic paper "Putting More on the Table: How Making Multiple Offers Can Increase the Final Value of the Deal," Victoria Medvec offers a compelling theory of multiple equivalent simultaneous offers (MESOs). Her research has shown that choice helps reveal what's most important to the other side. "MESOs allow you to secure an understanding of the other side's interests that we would be unlikely to ascertain through direct questioning," the paper asserts. "Through MESOs, we can detect whether one side might be misrepresenting his perspective or inadvertently overstating his position. MESOs are an effective strategy at the beginning, middle, and end of the negotiation, allowing us to constantly anchor, learn, detect, persist, and reframe."

Super Bowl XXVIII

Another example of turning a statement into a question comes from my first job offer in the sports world. Negotiating for the first job is one of the toughest challenges any of us face, because we are almost certainly going to have less experience than the person who offers the job. But like everyone, I had to start somewhere.

I desperately wanted to work at Super Bowl XXVIII in Atlanta, which was held in late January 1994 at the Georgia Dome. I was running out of money and didn't want to have to return to Michigan because I couldn't cut it in Atlanta. I wanted to prove myself, and the Super Bowl was my big employment goal. I doubt any of the NFL players preparing for the game were any more pumped up than I was to be part of this event.

When the call came from former Atlanta Falcons coach Leeman Bennett, I was ecstatic. I would be the liaison between him, the transportation committee, the NFL commissioner, and volunteers. In reality, that meant answering his phone 400 times a day—before cell phones.

"And we'll pay you six hundred a month," Bennett said.

"Okay," I replied, hung up, and called my parents.

I thought they'd be thrilled.

"Uh, Molly, you can't live on that," Dad said.

"Really?" I answered. It may sound funny, but I had been so focused on getting the job that the pay had been secondary. Bennett knew I would take anything, and my quick "okay" told him he was right.

Confronted with my dad's truth, I called Bennett back. I knew enough not to call him and whine that $600 wasn't enough to live on. I was smart enough to throw the medicine ball back to him in the form of a new assumption.

"That six hundred dollar salary you mentioned," I said. "That's per week, right?"

It was a pretty good try for a kid like me. I had to see if the truth would embarrass him and cause him to say, "Wow, you know, six hundred a month is crazy. Let's do twelve hundred." But of course Bennett knew the comps. He knew that every young adult my age would take that money and shut up, which was what I ended up doing.

The story makes me smile today because even though I was not successful in that salary negotiation, picking up the phone and going to bat for myself was an incredibly important rehearsal for the calls I would make all the time on behalf of professional athletes, coaches, and announcers. It's also important that you learn what I've learned: no tactic is going to work all the time in every negotiation. The point of this book is to equip you with tools that you can draw on to match your circumstance. Negotiating is about calling audibles the way a great quarterback does; he is always thinking on his feet, and even in situations of great uncertainty he is guiding the conversation with confidence.

I had rudimentary confidence when I picked up the phone to call Bennett, and even though he basically laughed at my "counter-offer," I had more experience that I could draw on for the next difficult call. You have to have a kernel of belief to make the ask; you become confident with more experience and success, which comes with practice.

When I said to Bennett, "That's per week, right?" I was giving him a choice between what he told me first (per month) and what I wanted (per week). Offering choice adds to your authority because it signals 360-Degree Awareness. Each choice should fit into a scenario that represents gains for you and the other side, in keeping with the other side's fears, desires, and motivation gained from Setting the Stage and Finding Common Ground.

The Power of You

In dealing with interpersonal relationships, we're often told to avoid starting questions with "you." In many situations, starting a sentence that way can seem threatening and provoke defensiveness.

In a negotiation, "you" can be a powerful tool for authority and one you should embrace. "It" or "I" is not going to get you where "you" will. "You" puts the focus on the other side and what it has and can do; it is a direct shot to the ego, and that's important to understand as you craft your ask. Reread my opening story about the antique store and notice that I never said "I." I used "my mom" and "we" and "you," in this case plural, because I was referring to both guys and looking at both of them when I said it.

A case in point about "you" involves my good friend Kathy Betty, who purchased the Atlanta Dream WNBA franchise by asking other investors to join her. She was reluctant despite her long career in finance as one of the first female partners at Ernst & Young and being near the top of the technology sector (her husband Garry founded EarthLink). The Dream deal involved an investment in which there were quite a few ambiguities and required a strong spirit of belief among investors and their basketball team that they would solve the uncertainties as they went forward.

From this delicate position, she settled on a strategy for her ask. She didn't sugarcoat it, and she tried to make this the first sentence of the ask: "If you invest in this, you have to be willing to lose your money," she told them (which is what more start-ups probably should say to their prospects). "Unless you're willing to lose this money, you don't need to listen to me any further." Her bold, targeted personal approach succeeded. She built trust and solidified her network. She found out as the deal unfolded that the investors she approached, many of them friends of hers, were actually honored that she asked them. She had no reason to fear, but her fear— as seasoned as she was—was normal.

One of my favorite examples of the power of using the second person "you" is Mark DeRosa. He is a supersmart middle infielder we signed to a $13 million deal with the Chicago Cubs at a time when the general manager, Jim Hendry, was making deals left and right.

This deal was more than Mark expected to ever make. ESPN. com reported: "Mark DeRosa became the first major league free agent to switch teams this offseason, agreeing Tuesday to a

$13 million, three-year contract with the Chicago Cubs. A nine-year veteran, he is expected to be the Cubs' everyday second baseman next season. The 31-year-old DeRosa batted a career-high .296 with 13 homers and a career-best 74 RBI last season for the Texas Rangers, appearing at six positions and starting at all four infield spots. He can also play the outfield."

The next day, his brother—a financial advisor—sent us a massive bouquet. "I can't thank you enough," he said in a follow-up phone call. "You've changed Mark's life forever."

In 20 years of deals like this, I had never heard a reaction quite like that of DeRosa's brother. Why was it so meaningful; why did it stand out? My conclusion: when the big athletes say anything about a deal, they almost always say, "I appreciate *it*." What I heard from the DeRosas was "I appreciate *you*."

That's a big difference. That was an arrow straight to my heart, and I recognized the value of that simple little word. "You" made all the difference. Too often we use "it" or "that" as a crutch. "It" is not specific and misses the chance to appeal to the ego and the power base of the other side.

Go for Face Time

Asking by phone or e-mail may be your only option and may seem desirable. We're in a time and culture in which our technology serves to connect and buffer us from one another; screens and headsets give us a sense of control and a comfortable distance.

If this is the first negotiation with the other side, if at all possible, I highly recommend making the ask in person. The awareness that you can have in person is invaluable because of nonverbal communication. You can collect the sort of data that supports the ability to better negotiate, but nonverbals can give you a sense of whether you should be the first to ask, which is rarely a bad thing. As with a coin flip in football, it's important to know how you will react either way. The first number is going to set one end of the negotiating range, and because the final result will probably move away from the initial ask, you will want to ask for more than you want. This is your anchor, and you want to drop it as deftly as possible. You can do that best in person.

In the antique store, I studied the tone and volume of the sellers' voices and the signs of anxiety or interest in their body language. There's no way I would have gotten those souvenirs for my mom by calling those guys. I had to make eye contact and connect in person for that deal to come off. It's so much easier for someone to feel aligned with you, to feel as if he or she and you are teammates, when the negotiation is done in person. It's a more vulnerable and powerful place where true connection, I would argue, is made.

The more you care about the negotiation, the more important it is to ask in person. Any time you go in for a raise or deal with an employee over money or family issues, all that should be done live. Yes, there is a risk of an adverse reaction, but this is another opportunity to turn defensiveness into curiosity. The information and data that you can collect in negotiations will help you in the long run, and you will collect a ton more in person.

Precise Often Means Concise

You have to find the language that you feel comfortable with; I advise you to Ask with Confidence in as few words as possible. In Chapter 1, I talked about my relationship with Ernie Johnson, the NBA broadcaster, one of the nicest guys in the business and a two-time Emmy winner as a studio host. Here's how I brokered a deal for him to handle the keynote speech for a company that was hosting a big conference.

We hashed out the particulars: a 45-minute speech, a question-and-answer period, 30 minutes of "grip and grin" photographs, and then he was done. EJ's such a nice guy that he would do this all day for free, but that's why he needs us: he needs to preserve time for his day job.

My tone was polite and confident to the company's representative: "His fee needs to start with a two and have at least five digits."

And it did.

PRACTICE

For me, it's not practice that makes perfect, it's practice of precision that makes perfect. What I've described above is my checklist for what and how I am going to ask. Practicing this is what gives me confidence. It didn't happen overnight and it doesn't guarantee success every time, but I know that by doing these steps I am in my best position as a negotiator.

Practice by Doing

You are probably already Asking with Confidence but may not be aware of it. One common negotiation in my world is establishing my fee with a new client.

Agents are paid a percentage of the contracts they negotiate for their clients. Unlike selling a printer or a pair of shoes, we are selling an intangible form of entertainment, not something you can touch and feel but something that carries the promise of an extraordinary experience. Standard industry fees are sometimes mandated by the unions. Major League Baseball fees are 4 percent of the player's contract, but the cut cannot result in a player making less than the league minimum. In the National Football League, the maximum fee has been reduced a couple of times over the years and is now 3 percent of the player's contract. There is no commission cap in the National Hockey League, but agents typically get a 4 percent fee from a player's contract. For college coaches (4 percent), broadcasters (10 percent), and golfers (20 percent), fees follow looser industry standard fees.

Why is there negotiation between players and agents? Some agents will cut their fees to gain clients. This is similar to what real estate agents do. I avoid this by working hard on the front end through Favor Columns and other aspects of Setting the Stage and Finding Common Ground. I can Ask with Confidence for my fee because I have met my objective: to have demonstrated so much value and created such a strong connection and so much clarity for the prospective client that the client feels the fee is fair. In 20 years and 300 clients, I have had fewer than a half-dozen who ever negotiated their fees with me. This is a testament to the connection that existed.

In the rare cases when clients push back on the fee, I view it as a great chance to demonstrate my work ethic. Every part of me knew that they were about to have their expectations far exceeded, and so I set a trial period in which I would prove the value of connecting toward a shared common goal. "How about we start here and if after six months you don't feel like it's fair, let's readdress it," I would say. "I'll even remind you." In six months, those few holdouts were persuaded of my value. Cutting my fee at that point, they knew, would be cutting me. I could push myself only this long before the fee would become difficult for my self-respect to keep absorbing, and I would lose motivation to keep up that level of service. The clients saw the value and agreed that I was worth the fee for which I (still) asked with confidence.

Expect Success

All dialogue in the course of negotiation can and should be used as practice for a confident ask.

As a sports agent, I not only Ask with Confidence on behalf of my client, but I communicate with confidence with my client at every step. A story about major league catcher Michael Barrett shows how this works and how much fun negotiating can be.

"What is your expectation of pay? How much do you want to get paid each season?" I asked him.

"Seven hundred thousand," he replied. "If you got me seven hundred, I would be pumped."

I knew we could do better—a lot better. We had comps above that. After several discussions with the team, we came to a firm deal. (Barrett, of course, wasn't in these meetings; we have greater success when the client's emotion and story are on paper, holding stable while the negotiation takes place.)

We called Barrett.

"Michael, what if we told you we have a deal at seven hundred thousand? What do you think?"

"Great! Wow. Really?" he replied.

"What if we told you we got eight hundred thousand? Would you be pumped?"

"Oh, yes," he said.

"What if we got to nine hundred thousand? How would you feel?"

"Wait, what is going on?"

"Okay, we . . ." I paused. "Got you one million."

He went nuts.

We could be confident asking him these rhetorical questions and having a little fun because we knew what we had. I like to reverse engineer this story. What if you knew you were going to negotiate a great deal like that every time? You would be confident in asking for what you knew was coming. That's the kind of confidence I'm talking about: asking with the understanding and expectation that the terms will be given to you.

This story also illustrates that managing expectations is huge. Often we have the urge and vision to be the hero, especially to someone who is counting on us to deliver. It's easy to overpromise. Managing expectations as part of Finding Common Ground is so important because it means that the ask is not a stretch. Over-promising creates a climate of pressure that can choke confidence.

A Study in Confidence: Francoeur

In Chapter 1, I used Jeff Francoeur as an example of the importance of knowing the other side as you are Setting the Stage. The story of his salary negotiation is also one of Asking with Confidence.

We knew the Atlanta Braves wanted to avoid the same thing we did—arbitration—and we were working against a ticking clock. Their side was changing the trigger person—the one to whom we were making the ask. That could have flustered and frustrated us, but instead those factors combined to help us Ask with Confidence on behalf of Francoeur. The other side's inconsistency helped us be more consistent. At the heart of our side was Francoeur, who was nothing if not confident.

As a rookie, Francoeur made the cover of *Sports Illustrated*, which proclaimed him "the Natural." He grew up in the suburbs

of Atlanta, where he led his high school team to the state championship and was good enough in football to turn down a big scholar-
ship. People thought of him as the Man, their darling, he who could
do no wrong. He had no problem filling that role. He was hand-
some, even dashing in his aggressive at-bats and chatter with the
fans in right field (even the ones at hostile ballparks). He was gutsy
and believed in himself. But from his first day in the big leagues to
about his third year, he was paid the mandated minimum salary;
the team renewed him for about $425,000 a year because it could.
It had no reason to pay him more.

Everyone knew Francoeur would be up for a sizable deal once
he was eligible for arbitration. That meant that he could reject the
Braves' deal and ask a panel of impartial judges to determine the fairness of the offer. The arbitrators' decision is binding, and so there's
a lot at stake in that environment, and as much aggressive risk taking as there is in pro sports, very few players and teams want to go to
arbitration. It's almost like family members who go to court; there's
never going to be a great long-term resolution after an experience
like that.

When the Braves offered approximately $25 million each to
Francoeur and catcher Brian McCann, his Little League teammate
who had grown up in his big shadow, Francoeur turned the team
down. (Meanwhile McCann, who as a catcher took much more
physical punishment each game than Francoeur, accepted the deal.
He told me later that it was just the package he needed to settle in
Atlanta, where his family and heart were at that time in his career).

"Dude, I will make more money on comps year to year than
settling on a long-term deal," was Francoeur's attitude. He wanted
to bet on himself playing better every year. We like to say that a
guy like him has the balls to roll the dice. Looking back, he should
have taken the deal that McCann accepted. But that was Francoeur

for you. We honored his confidence as we made our ask for a one-year contract. "I'm not taking under $3.225 million," he had told us. We asked for $3.95 million.

Francoeur also wanted certain sweeteners, which we felt were fair asks, such as bonuses for a certain number of runs batted in, plate appearances, those kinds of statistics. The Braves had never been crazy about his statistics, but Francoeur felt strongly that certain bonus numbers would motivate him to achieve better baseball statistics. We had great trust in Francoeur's ability, which added to our confidence.

After many asks and counteroffers and several back-and-forths, we were getting closer but not close enough. "We've got to get him the bonuses so he's protected when he has a hell of a year," I told general manager Frank Wren, who had originally offered $2.8 million.

Not long afterward Wren called me back. "We are flying to Phoenix for arbitration," he threatened. "If you don't like our offer, see you there."

Here's the thing: Asking with Confidence means staying confident even after the ask. I did. I stuck with my numbers, just as I do when I am at a store and deal with a salesperson. "I'm going to need X, Y, or Z," I say with a smile. I'm nice. I'm not a bitch, but my tone makes it clear that I'm serious.

I drew confidence from knowing that the team wanted what Francoeur did, although for a different reason. We wanted to avoid arbitration because we didn't want Francoeur in front of three impartial mediators who wouldn't be permitted to weigh his pull in the Atlanta market. These three people would work solely from baseball numbers, and we didn't want this trio of strangers deciding his future.

Ultimately, it was sticking with our number and riding out the clock that helped us get the best contract for Francoeur. We agreed to terms on a one-year, $3.375 million contract with a laundry list of bonuses. We had Set the Stage, Found Common Ground, and Asked with Confidence.

Practice a Confident Tone

So much of what we communicate isn't in words but in the way those words are carried. Tone is critically important. It can be hard to judge our own best tone for making a confident ask; I often advise young negotiators to find a trusted advisor who can and will give them honest feedback on tone. It is something you know when you hear or feel it. You signal so much through a tone, whether it is loud or soft, fast or slow. Just watch a basketball coach on the sidelines.

Generally, I use a faster tone to signal eagerness and passion and a slower, quiet tone to communicate control and calm. I want my tone, not just my words, to validate the other side and reinforce my self-confidence. I want to be listened to, so I first want to establish a feeling and atmosphere that says I will be an empathetic listener. I know that the model I set can help the other side see a secure path to follow when it is unsure, and that's important because there is a lot of uncertainty in negotiation. I aim for a tone that's going to assure the other side that I can get it out of this situation no matter what and I don't bite.

I would argue that tone gains importance when the ask becomes more personal. I've had to practice my most effective negotiating tones on flights with my family. In Chapter 2 you learned how I use coupons to build Favor Columns with fellow passengers; what is critical for me in that situation and in my story about the antiques for my mom is the tone. It's as important as or more important than the precise wording of the ask.

The airplane is a tough situation because my family is there with me, we're spread out, and I'm trying to negotiate with strangers so our five can sit together. It's a place that literally has very little space to move around, and the people I care about the most are banking that I'll deliver. When my girls were under age 10, that was when they most wanted to sit next to me, and of course I felt the same way.

"Can you do me a huge favor?" I ask a fellow passenger whose seat is next to mine. "I've got my girls with me, and my seat is in the economy comfort section. By any chance would you consider sitting there?"

Tone and timing, as much as words, are the keys in this cramped environment. I make my tone soft and enthusiastic. My body language is approachable and appropriate. It's not a statement; that would sound entitled. I want to ask them with respect and expectation, to guide them to a better place—better because they know they've helped me and my kid sit together and because my seat is in a better spot on the plane.

This careful, relaxed tone is what I use when I check into a hotel and prefer the single king bed over the two doubles that are in my assigned room.

"Hey, how are you?" I ask the front desk person. "Thanks so much for checking me in."

I know from years of business travel that these people are used to getting their ears bent by high-maintenance guests. They very rarely hear genuine compliments. I won't say thank you if they didn't seem to care to begin with, but most of them do and are willing to serve or they would not be in this line of work. Tone as much as anything will help you draw out their most giving nature. Over time, with practice, you will find your most effective tone in each situation. Often there is trial and error with tone and the shifts that are natural as negotiations evolve. You may well switch your tone when the other side counteroffers or find, as I do, that keeping the same tone is a way to telegraph consistency in your position. If you are working on a negotiation team, discuss your tone and rehearse it before the ask. Don't assume that there is one tone that fits every negotiation. That's a big mistake. As with conversations, negotiations have an organic flow that you will begin to notice and react to well. When in doubt about the right tone, trust your intuition.

Hone Your Timing

Timing the ask is critical to getting the yes. I would argue that the timing of the ask can determine the outcome. The more you have at stake, the more you need to make sure your timing is excellent. Think of the person at the bar who upon meeting you proposes marriage. What else can you think but "Freak!" Time is a necessary element in creating a bond strong enough to sustain an ask. Timing demonstrates that you understand the other side exquisitely and are authentically seeking the best opening to make the deal work. It signals a mutual connection or at least a strong desire to make one happen.

Here are some questions that help me clarify that the right time to ask is approaching:

1. Have I clearly delivered outstanding value already?
2. Have I clearly articulated what we do and how we do what we do?
3. Have I connected, not just communicated, with the other side?
4. Has it interacted with me?
5. Has it asked questions?

6. Has it been at least fairly responsive when I reach out to it?

7. Has it taken the favors I have offered?

We've all experienced the sour taste of asking too early and getting rejected or not asking at the right time and missing the opportunity. It doesn't feel good. An example of great timing involved Jeff Francoeur. After almost two years of recruiting him, building a Favor Column, and helping him, the timing was getting right to sign him. Baseball players are tendered a contract in mid-December, and if it is tendered through an agent, the agent most certainly has rights to the fees for that year's deal. Therefore, it was important to me that we were able to sign Jeff before the tender deadline so that we could capture the fees. When he told me he was planning to head down to his place in Florida for a couple of days, I knew we would miss the window. I went into solution mode, offering to fly him down on our plane, have dinner that night, execute the deal, and have all of us celebrate with a champagne toast on the beach. Phew! Timing is about finding the best window through which the best answer can find you.

The following are methods that I use to make an ask. The first is to roll out my "go" plan, which is bringing to life what I am going to do when they say go. This is a vibrant description of details of how, when, where, and so on. "You ready to go?" is the simple way I end my ask.

The second is more low-key: "So my thinking is if you can execute this contract, we can run with ABC tomorrow, which is so important for us to be able to do XYZ." ABC and XYZ are vibrant descriptions of what I know the client wants to see happen; ABC is short-term action that we can jump on immediately, and XYZ is a longer-term outcome of those actions. This language creates a sense of urgency around the action that I want the other side to take. It is both precise and practiced.

Practice Not Taking Anything Personally

I didn't want Francoeur, Barrett, or any of my pro athletes, coaches, or broadcasters present when I negotiated for them. These are high performers whose egos must stay healthy and confident; the last thing they need is for their employer to bash them in person. But negotiating can get that way, and as an agent, I am the stand-in for the talent. It's a heck of a lot easier for me to absorb the abuse, because it's about my client, not me.

Even so, although negotiations usually center on financial figures and other numbers, at the heart of the back-and-forth are people—real people. A successful negotiator never forgets this. There is never a deal in which you can't try to inject some warmth and humanity into the proceedings. It is important to separate the humans from the numbers and details, to know that the relationships are foremost even if the deal cannot be struck. Not taking anything personally means that you have the maturity to step outside of the ask, outside of the deal, and get a longer view of what the actions mean. A negotiation centers on a problem that involves people, and if you can work together to find a mutually beneficial answer (by Setting the Stage and Finding Common Ground), the problem is no longer so personal. It can even be a launching pad for mutual success. When both sides can explore the other's interests and not be stuck on their respective bottom lines, some great problem solving can happen—and some incredible long-term relationships can form.

Not taking it personally is a habit that can and should be practiced in all aspects of life so that it becomes a natural reflex in negotiations. Despite the fact that our culture is so me-centered (we all know our share of narcissists), we become so much better at negotiating when we can have a Teflon spirit with others. Practice using these moments of perceived criticism as a chance to gain information and ask questions. This elasticity will promote patience and confidence as you move to and around the ask and toward a resolution.

Circling back to the antique store where this chapter began, I remember with fondness my mom's reaction when the print and the flower arrangement were delivered to her bed-and-breakfast.

"No way!" she said, delighted. And I shared that with her. Negotiating well is a gift with the power to ripple into so many lives and make such a great difference. For me, these items showed my willingness to go to bat for my mom with my professional skills. Asking with Confidence can be demonstrated with far more at stake in your world once you have practiced making a precise ask to the point where you have no doubt or fear. By now, you should be feeling more comfortable with these building blocks of negotiation as we move into another critical skill: Embracing the Pause.

SUMMARY

Making the ask is the point in negotiating that makes people most uncomfortable and fearful. If you have carefully laid the groundwork by Setting the Stage and Finding Common Ground, your ask will be expected. A confident ask is precise and time-sensitive. The more you practice, the better you will get at Asking with Confidence. Remember, you have already added value, built a strong connection, and created clarity. Now you can Ask with Confidence.

Asking with Confidence is accomplished through the following habits:

- **Counter fear with positive self-talk.** An optimistic mental script helps drown out the fear that keeps most people from asking.

- **Remember the Ps.** Precision + practice = confidence. Practice of precision makes perfect. Success isn't guaranteed each time, but the more you practice these steps, the better positioned you will be as a negotiator.

- **Ask for what you want.** Move away from asking for *what you think you will get* or what the other side *won't mind giving you.* Know exactly what you want and frame your ask around specifics.

- **Choice is always relevant.** Precision doesn't mean narrowness. Offer choice to improve your chances for success. Choice offers a sense of control and mutual benefit.

- **Tap the power of "you."** Embrace the second person point of view. "You" appeals to the ego and power base, putting the focus on the other side and what it has and can do.

- **Go for face time.** If this is a first negotiation or a negotiation that is highly important to you, make the ask in person if at all possible.

- **Expect success.** Ask as if you know you'll succeed. Managing expectations is key; overpromising can choke confidence.

- **Watch your tone.** Much of what we communicate isn't in words but in how those words are said. Practice your most effective tone; it may differ with the situation.

- **Never take it personally.** Negotiations may center on figures, but people are at the core. Being emotionally flexible will help you move toward resolution.

4

Embracing the Pause

"Is he still there?" my husband whispered as I held my phone to my ear.

It was almost midnight, and we had been asleep. I get work calls all the time. I buy pajamas with pockets in them for my cell phone. Negotiations don't respect the nine-to-five workday.

I muted the phone, but I was still whispering.

"Yes!"

I couldn't blame Fred for asking. For several long, long, looooong seconds, only silence had come from the phone speaker.

On the other end of the call was Atlanta Braves general manager Frank Wren. The last thing I had said was that my ask on behalf of Jeff Francoeur was firm.

This was the pause between the ask and what we were both trying to avoid: arbitration. The longer the seconds stretched out, the more I felt that we would get what we had asked for, and the more I felt that he wanted to get this done.

The seconds kept ticking. The minutes followed one another, the way they do when you watch an accident unfold. They take on bigger space in a negotiation, too. In that space, I could sense that Frank might expect me to cave in to relieve the uncertainty.

I tried to relax. I definitely wasn't going to say anything. My whole outlook was to stay firm and comfortable. That is what this chapter is about: Embracing the Pause.

More often than not, no matter how well the negotiations are going, there will be a point when you reach some sort of stalemate. You might be just short of a breakthrough, but the sides haven't been able to reach mutually agreeable deal points. This is the time to Embrace the Pause.

Embracing the Pause may look like doing nothing, but in this chapter I will demonstrate its deep power. In reality, pausing to do nothing is doing everything to help you negotiate.

Pausing allows you to listen, and when you listen, you learn.

WHAT THE PAUSE ACCOMPLISHES

The pause may be only as long as a breath, or it can be any length of time before the next communication. Most of us feel uncomfortable with dead zones in conversation. A conversation—and that's what a negotiation boils down to—is like a tightrope stretched between two people. Silence makes you look around for the net, some sort of signal that we are still in communication and nothing has gone wrong.

We don't like ambiguity. It's a big vacuum, and we try to fill it. In a conversation or negotiation, silence can signal ambiguity.

In that discomfort, we seek to fill the space with small talk— anything that can make us feel that we are still in a safe place with the other person. Some professions take full advantage of the human need to break for a pause. Two groups of people who will never interrupt you and will always expect you to fill the silence are attorneys and the media. Attorneys get paid by the hour, so the more you talk, the more they make. The reporters and journalists who have crossed my path know that the more information they have, the better the story. The more their source speaks, the greater the chance is of that person saying something noteworthy or even sensational.

Both lawyers and the media are criticized heavily in our culture, but that's a tribute to their ability to use what we say to their greatest benefit. They have mastered the art of quiet, and in that space they give us every chance to help them. We can learn from them to be better negotiators by Embracing the Pause the way they do.

To illustrate the power of the pause in the extreme case, I think most of us have experienced that grace of closeness with those who are closest to us. We do not fear the silence of intimacy because we know one another so well that this level of silence is safe. We have this understanding of silence whenever we rock a child to sleep or spend time with someone who is injured and cannot speak. In everyday life, with people we don't know as well, we are right to fear the pause because we associate silence with uncertainty.

I see this with my daughters. Like most kids, they would rather play than clean their rooms.

"It needs to be spotless before we leave for church," I tell them.

"But Mom," they reply, and whatever they say next is just more blah, blah, blah to me.

They keep talking. I stay quiet.

I pause. I stare at them. I'm telegraphing to them that this isn't a six-minute mile I'm asking for, but if they don't get their behinds up the stairs in a minute, they will be running laps around the house.

They don't hear that. They don't hear anything. They just know that when I'm quiet, they have reason to fear. I stand my ground, and it doesn't take long for them to finally end their excuses because they're not getting anywhere and they've started to get in touch with the fear wrapped in my silence.

I'm still pausing as they turn and run up the stairs to do what I've asked them (and Asked with Confidence because I knew they could manage this task).

I'm not advocating negotiating from a place of fear, only noting that this emotion is part of the dynamic with my children. My point is that in negotiation, the moment of quiet between the ask and the answer is a chance to think and reflect, to control the negotiation, to balance and move toward one side, sometimes to build anxiety, and most of all for you to send the message that you are very comfortable with yourself.

NOT ALL AT ONCE

My comfort level with the pause comes from the knowledge gained over time that very rarely in negotiations is there a point where everything happens all at once. We tend to think that it will, partly because we think we want it to. In reality, negotiations are often a long, protracted dance of many steps. When I talk about Asking with Confidence, that can mean multiple asks as the other side responds. This pattern means that there will be multiple pauses as well.

When you reach a point where you know that an entire deal is not going to happen all at once, you can breathe and relax. You are not in fight or flight mode, ready to sprint across the savannah to escape a lion or catch a zebra barehanded for your next meal. You may feel tight because you want the deal to close, perhaps because you have financial pressures or career goals at stake.

That urgency is not your friend. The other side can sense it, and it never feels right. It telegraphs to them that they should be worried, too. You know what it's like to be sold too hard on a car or a house or some sort of precious merchandise; pushiness can be verbal or nonverbal, and it is always a red flag.

DIALING BACK URGENCY

In earlier chapters, I showed how urgency works in your favor. By responding in a timely fashion, you build a Favor Column and create 360-Degree Awareness. After the ask, the urgency that you may have channeled to the other side needs to be dialed back. The difference is that you always want to be urgent to the person on the other side but not to the deal that is between you. This is a key distinction.

Adding value to negotiation happens through the buildup to the ask, the timely work done by you to build the relationship. When you become urgent after making the ask, that often telegraphs confusion and pressure to the other side. You may be very anxious about its next move, but antsy behavior does not belong in a negotiation.

Urgency can be avoided through a holistic approach to your entire business, not a single negotiation. Although we are focused on negotiating in this book, this process probably coexists with other relationships and duties in your job. A balanced approach to negotiation is reflected in a balanced approach to work. Unless your work is totally focused on one big deal after another, it's important to have a steady pipeline of deals that require you to spread your attention. As you have prospects in different phases of the negotiation cycle and the negotiations close at various phases, you can switch gears often and avoid the urgency of pressing on one negotiation.

Another way to think about this stage in negotiating is to visualize the way a community pool works. Where I swim, for a certain portion of each hour the kids must leave the pool. Everything is calm during "adult swim." Embracing the Pause is your version of adult swim, and building it into your negotiation process and style is a sign of maturity.

WHY SHUT UP?

A constant talker can be frustrating to the other side because the chatter fills the space and filtering what is important becomes intensive and annoying. Sure, there are people who use this tactic as a way to get what they want, because the other side just wants them to go away. It is the negotiating equivalent of an attorney who drowns the other side with paperwork and filings in an attempt to wear them down and make the lawsuit go away.

Talking to fill the space in negotiation is not the way to build solid, long-term relationships. No one really wants to do business with a chatterbox. Such people may have to do business with you, but they won't like it. A big part of long-term success in negotiation is demonstrating consistency, honesty, and integrity. It's not just about this deal; your deal today is a stepping-stone to bigger, better, and more meaningful deals in the future.

At the point of making the ask, talking a lot is damaging for other reasons. You can come off as a know-it-all, especially if you fill the silence with a dissection of the other side's options. Taken to an extreme, reviewing options after making the ask can come off as a threat. It sounds almost funny, but this is like a gangster movie in which the tough guy snarls, "So, what's it gonna be?" and the hero is squirming between a rock and a hard place.

Don't stereotype or pigeonhole yourself; if anything, channel a relaxed coolness, knowing that you have set up this negotiation and communicated your ask the best way you know how on the basis of the homework you've done with this client. There's no reason not to feel that you can carry over this confidence into the pause.

Talking at this stage of the negotiation can also signal that you are lacking confidence or that you are extremely nervous. Perhaps your chatter is a tactic to hide any opportunity for the other side to ask a tough question.

When I am in a negotiation with someone who talks incessantly, all kinds of red flags go up. In contrast, I admire those who can live comfortably in the waiting time.

Most of us fall somewhere in between, and that's where a lot of improvement can be made in your negotiations.

Here are a few questions that can help you drill into why you may be the type of person who wants to talk after making an ask. The questions are also designed to help you dial back:

1. Are you someone who naturally wants to keep talking when others pause?

2. What is motivating you to fill the silence? If it is discomfort, why?

3. What benefit do you and others derive from having you filling the silence?

4. Going forward, what specific word, image, or role model can you turn to as a reminder of silence?

I love the last question, because images can be incredibly powerful in helping us change behavior and build values.

If I had to pick one off the top of my head, it would be the "speak no evil" monkey because speaking at this point in the negotiation is not going to do any good.

THE SQUIRM FACTOR

Whereas I have learned to Embrace the Pause, as an agent I have always had new clients who were not so seasoned. For many, a pro contract represented more money than they had ever seen or imagined. Yet would it be enough? What would the future hold? What if they got injured or went into a slump? Especially if they haven't yet made "enough money for a lifetime," most are scared. What if this deal goes away? Then what do I do?

These are very real questions for many superstars who come from limited means. I often represent them as they negotiate their biggest deals, and I have to sell them on the idea of Embracing the Pause, often by modeling it for them. (This is another reason why Setting the Stage and Finding Common Ground are such important steps for creating trust and helping them understand that I have a great sense and command of the deal.)

It's often easier for them to see examples of the power of the pause in their world. Time-outs and pauses are part of most sports. We talk with admiration about the baseball batter who is patient at the plate, who with the eye of a jeweler expands the milliseconds of each pitch, forcing the pitcher to earn the out—or give up a hit. In football, basketball, and hockey, a time-out is a strategic limited tool for coaches to try to change the momentum of the game or throw off the other team, especially a kicker who is about to try a game-winning field goal.

Individual sports treat stoppages differently. Think about the front-runner who pauses just a second to look back at the competition, only to see them blow by. In golf, players who pause too much are given warnings and fines because their actions are counter to the fair play of the game. A golfer can't afford to embrace that kind of pause.

You can look across music, writing, comedy, and many other fields to see how pauses are used strategically to create specific effects and communicate with precision. One of the most famous examples is the signage at every London subway station: "Mind the gap," referring to the space between the train and the platform, which must be crossed with some care to ensure safety. All these examples show the power of stopping even for a second and how that can change your environment. Paying attention to that power is the first step toward tapping it.

The pause is very difficult for people who have fears and anxiety about the outcome. In this vacuum, they struggle mightily to find some sort of trust, some shred of belief. My role is to talk them through this: "Trust me. Be patient. It's the first offer. Sit tight; we'll get there."

FINDING YOUR OWN INSPIRATION

Because we live in a time when people rush so much, our daily lives work against the practice of Embracing the Pause. It's important to look for other ways that this strategy works in our daily lives so that we can incorporate it into negotiating.

One way to help you identify and appreciate the power of the pause is through music. Songs that resonate with us usually feature strategic pauses that create emotional effects for listeners.

Identify a song that creates a strong emotional memory for you and describe why that happens. What is it about that memory that means so much to you?

Now listen to the song twice. Each time, pay attention to any pauses or shifts in the tempo, lyrics, or volume. What dramatic effect is created through those pauses?

The other practice that I advocate is to incorporate silence into daily conversations. Here are some suggestions to help guide you in that habit. Jot down an example of pausing when you wanted to keep talking.

In that space, what did you learn or gain? How did the decision to stop talking affect the conversation in the short term and the long term? What happened in the space created by your silence? Did you recognize nonverbal messages from the others who took part in your conversation? Was it uncomfortable for you, and if so, how did you manage that ambiguity?

CREATING ANTICIPATION

Anticipation is one of my favorite words. I use it with my daughters constantly. Think about what's going to happen next. A pause is an opportunity for creating anticipation, and anticipation is a great antidote for uncertainty. I think of anticipation as having clarity around where a conversation is going.

Watching pro golfers is a great way to appreciate this aspect of the pause. So much of their sport is about managing the downtime between shots. I have been fortunate enough to walk inside the ropes with my clients as they compete, and that opportunity has given me a close-up view of how they use downtime to build anticipation.

On a par-five hole, for example, they hit their drives, and they have a 300-yard walk (ideally down the fairway because they've hit it long and straight). As they begin to move, they have already collected data that may change by the time they get to the ball. They are looking at the wind and what it might be doing to the tops of the trees, not just at the spot where they are now standing. They are considering their options of not just making the next shot but where that properly executed shot will take them. They are in the moment, and they are also calculating the possibilities of the next moment. This may sound complicated, and believe me, when these guys were starting out, they weren't at this level of mental ability. Their assessments must be made in keeping with the pace of play and in consideration of other factors beyond their control, such as crowd noise. Sometimes they have to troubleshoot on the spot when the ball ends up in a tough lie. I love watching how they anticipate and keep the flow of performance in the face of so many factors. It inspires me to do the same thing when I am negotiating their contracts.

In baseball, I've watched pitchers work batters the same way. There's a calculated strategy for each batter that the pitcher and catcher have worked out on the basis of past experience. (They have worked to Set the Stage and Find Common Ground; each pitch is an ask for the batter to swing.) If a pitcher knows a batter will sit until he gets a fastball, the pitcher is going to throw his best setup. He is going to try to fill that space, that pause, with a slower pitch that clips the strike zone. The pitchers who last longest and have the most success are usually versatile, which is another important trait for negotiators as well.

Anticipation builds on the knowledge of possible outcomes. You can build anticipation through the pause intentionally and practice your strategy. The pause is a time to consider what's next in your scope of possibilities and practice your next precise move. A great example in sports are the coaches who break down game films before the next game so that they can envision as many scenarios as possible and guide the team to practice accordingly. Anticipation creates efficiency, limits errors, decreases surprises, and often gives you a better chance of conducting a successful negotiation.

Here are some points I review as much as possible when there is a pause in the negotiation:

- What are the other side's greatest fears?
- Are there events and issues happening now in its world that can affect this negotiation?

- What sources are most influential to the other side (personal networks, social media, industry news)? Am I keeping up as much as possible with its news feed?

Because past behavior predicts future actions, I review what I have experienced with this person that defines his or her values, goals, and style. I ask myself the following questions:

- How might those past actions play a part in this negotiation and our ongoing relationship?

- What are my assets and liabilities going forward? They can be positive (resources, product, personality) or negative (anxiety, pressure, price).

The answers to these questions help me create a visualization exercise. I imagine as fully as possible, with as many details as I can, what success would look like with this person. I know from the athletes and top performers with whom I work closely that the more vivid, realistic, and repeated I can make these visualizations, the more benefit I derive from them. I know that my mind cannot tell the difference between a real negotiation and a rehearsed one, and the more I rehearse success, the more I am poised for it.

The best way to do this is by unplugging, relaxing, and taking a few minutes to let your mind open. I often visualize the other side responding in various ways and how I will react. I identify points that might be conflicts and rehearse my reactions to them.

All this helps me get ready for the response from the other side. I am poised to listen for what I want to hear, and when I do, I am going to grab it and go. I am not going to ask questions or do favors. You will not hear me say, "Are you sure?" When I hear people say that, I think they don't really want what they say they want. That's not me. Precision is the place I come from.

These short, focused mental exercises help me in several ways. They relieve any anxiety, build confidence, and create anticipation for my next move in the negotiation. The fear in negotiation is real, and visualization can be a great tool to face it down and replace it with self-assured calm.

DATE NIGHT PAUSE

I recently had a date night with Fred. We laugh because it's not like we're party animals. We're the geeky couple who goes out early and gets home early because our family runs on an early schedule. That schedule isn't very negotiable at this point.

It's Friday, and we're at a great restaurant in one of the country's top spots for good food: Atlanta's Buckhead district, where actors and other celebrities like to dine, as do athletes and other superstars. For us it's not far away, and on this night we decide to try a spot popular with the young and hip. We didn't think we needed a reservation at 6 p.m.

We walk in. The restaurant seats about 50 people tops. About half the tables are full.

"Just two," Fred says.

"Do you have a reservation?" the host says. His smile is gritty, as if his answer is already no.

"No, we don't," Fred replies.

"So what does my last name need to be for me to have a reservation for two?" I ask jokingly. I am completely kidding.

The host smiles. That was the pause and nonverbal cue I needed.

"We don't have a famous last name, but we will be quick and tip well."

The guy is warming up. "You can sit at the bar," he says.

Now the pause is mine. I don't say anything. I just look at him. My face carries tremendous disappointment. The pause lengthens.

"We never get to do this, or at least not as much as we would like," I said. "We're excited to get a sense of this place. It's somewhere I could see us coming often because it's so close to our house."

Another pause. I keep my gaze fixed on him.

He looks back down at his podium, at the diagram of table assignments. Then he looks up.

"Okay, Susie, take them to table fifteen."

I smile. "Thanks tons," I tell him. "I'll make sure we don't back you up."

We ended up having a great meal at the pace we enjoy, not fast but not leisurely. It was perfect. Yes, it took some professional skills to get a good seat. You can see in this story how I used pauses to my advantage in this conversation to reinforce my position. There was also humor and an understanding of his world and what he was up against. I played to what I felt could and should be his desire to welcome local diners who could become regulars. I didn't take his first offer but held my ground for what I wanted.

Each of those pauses made my question carry greater weight. By doing that, I made it harder for him to turn me down.

PAUSING THROUGHOUT NEGOTIATION

The most important time to Embrace the Pause is after Asking with Confidence. Keep in mind, however, that pauses can be created throughout a negotiation to benefit you.

When I am Setting the Stage and Finding Common Ground, I am asking as many questions as possible. Some of these questions are difficult. For instance, when I have built a relationship with someone who already has an agent, at some point I need to ask a tough question so that we are both clear on where we stand. I totally cut to the chase.

"You happy with your agent?" I will ask. Yes, it's heavy. It's a turning point. It's just shy of the, "Will you go out with me?" question that starts every dating relationship.

When I ask this question or another heavy question, I'm interested not only in *what* they say but in *how* they say it. It's such a key question for me that I imagine it almost like a photograph framed by seconds and minutes. I want it to hang there between us.

I create that time by asking . . . and then stopping. I never say, "Ya know . . ." or "Umm. . . ."

Heavy questions and well-timed questions like the ones I asked the restaurant host function like medicine balls. These giant heavy balls are a tool that athletes used to use condition themselves, and boot camps have brought them back into popularity. You can't juggle, bounce, or play with a medicine ball. A heavy question is the same way, and you have to treat it like that. You throw it and it alone. You stop and wait for the answer. It's a lot to handle.

What can I tell from what and how those from the other side respond? If they reply quickly and firmly with no filler words, I can tell they were ready for the question and are clear on their answer. If they juggle the question or maybe even drop the ball, I can tell they are not so clear. They may even throw the medicine ball back to me. I sponge up all the clues from their behavior that can help me understand how they are thinking. Does the other side appear anxious? Eager? Does it return calls quickly? Does it initiate or wait? How long is long to it?

These clues are not one size fits all. Each depends on the person, because not everyone communicates the same way. These are general observations built over two decades of experience in negotiations, and within your unique world you will begin to tease out some critical information by Embracing the Pause as I have.

That big heavy question, that big ball, is in the hands of the other side, and it has to figure out what to do with it. You must create that space and stage for it to act and wait for an answer. The way it handles that big question is your gold in its rawest form. That moment tells you what you can do for it.

Frame the heaviest questions with a confident pause and plenty of patience. Know that as long as you build your pauses with expectation and not arrogance, they can be a powerful tool.

AVOIDING ARROGANCE

The challenge of Embracing the Pause is to do it without sending a message of arrogance. The last thing I want is to make the other side think that I am holding something back. This chapter is an extension of Chapter 3, because Embracing the Pause is the immediate transition from Asking with Confidence. I want to move seamlessly from the ask to the pause, and everything I do and say points to that goal.

The best way to avoid arrogance is by making the ask in person (I know this is not always possible). As a huge believer in the power of nonverbals, I try to ask with confidence and embrace the pause by keeping in mind these three parameters:

- I keep my chin parallel to the ground. I never lift it, because in our culture that is a subtle sign that I regard myself as more important than the person to whom I am speaking.
- I am careful to smile in a genuine manner and keep my gaze steady.
- I relax my face and muscles to ensure that I'm not displaying an aggressive posture and don't look like I am dissecting them.

All my physical actions are intended to project that I am comfortable with where I am. This is a small but important element in my overall aim to invite the other side to where I am comfortable, to make it feel that it will share that comfort as a result of a positive negotiation.

No one wants to give anything to someone who is cold and aloof, not if he or she doesn't have to. You may close the deal, but in the long run you will lose the business. It is important to make the other side aware that you care and you are passionate and want to win and that you don't mind engaging in pressured situations.

People want to be around a person who has the confidence to want the ball on the last play of the game, who can guide them through a tough deal. The aim is to make pressure into pleasure, which introverts especially have a hard time doing sometimes. If that's you, remember that confidence is built on the successful completion of smaller tasks. Getting comfortable with the pause earns you the respect and reliance that lead to a great negotiation and an ongoing relationship in business and beyond.

PRACTICE PAUSING THROUGH LOW-STAKES NEGOTIATING

While on a business trip, I discovered I had left my toothbrush at home. I called from my hotel room to the front desk to have them run up a replacement. It was a nice hotel, and I expected this service to be complimentary. I wasn't expecting a negotiation.

"I'm happy to grab one from our store and charge it to your room," she told me. "It's two dollars fifty, I believe."

I remained silent.

"Ma'am, are you there?" she said, and I knew the pause was working in my favor. It had turned her voice from edgy to concerned.

Business travelers get nickel and dimed a lot like this, and on principle I pushed back.

"Wow, I travel a lot, and typically the front desk is happy to bring up something like this, complimentary," I replied. "Would you maybe do that for someone you wanted to come back and stay with you again?"

"Okay, ma'am, I'll have it brought up, no charge," she said.

It was only $2.50, but the pause is just as effective when there are more zeros at stake. Practice at low stakes as much as you can to make the pause a go-to tool when you negotiate.

PUT YOURSELF IN THE UPPER DECK

The pause is the part of the negotiation in which I remove myself verbally and move myself mentally. I have spent most of the negotiation getting as close to the other side as I can as I Set the Stage and went about Finding Common Ground. Now it's time to step back and put myself in what I call the upper deck.

In a ballpark or stadium, the upper deck is the seats farthest away from the field of play. They are usually the cheapest seats and not ones that anyone would prefer. After I have Asked with Confidence, the upper deck is exactly where I want to be because being close to the action is not going to help me or the other side.

Creating distance at this point in the negotiation allows me to make sure I don't have any undue emotion about the outcome that is going to negatively influence the other side. By moving to the upper deck, I have a new, wider lens on what is at stake. I can't see as many details, but I can still see the big picture. It forces me to reframe the negotiation less personally and more factually. Remember that emotion is usually going to get in your way during a negotiation; this is most true after you have Asked with Confidence. Call it the upper deck or quiet time, but it's the space you need to get a different view of all the action so far and process it to your greatest benefit.

BEWARE OF ONLINE PAUSES

Another reason that I like to Ask with Confidence in person is that I know better where I stand and can verify the pause as beneficial to me. Communicating in any manner that is not face-to-face means that I cannot tap into this information. I am losing the chance to gauge hesitancy, energy level, tone, and timing.

When given the chance to use as many senses as possible to communicate, I don't want to give up the one that is arguably the most important: the ability to see the person on the other side. Also, I want that person to see me and understand the confidence, enthusiasm, and attitude of mutual benefit that I work hard to convey. In person, I am guided by the words of Maya Angelou: "I've learned that people will forget what you said, people will forget what you did, but people will never forget how you made them feel." Assuming you have a choice, do everything you can to narrow the distance between you and the other side.

Take a step back and look at the big picture of what's happening. We embrace technology as the way we do business and do it faster and in many ways better than ever, but its place in negotiation must be strategically considered. I have told Millennials who come to me for mentoring that they should not negotiate by e-mail unless they don't care if the deal happens at all. That may sound strong, and in some cases it may be extreme. The more there is at stake, the more you risk by negotiating without getting to read the other side in person.

Communication such as e-mail has a pause built in. Hit the send button and you have to wait for someone to reply. I don't know too many people who negotiate by chat or instant messaging, but that can make the pauses shorter. There is still distance and lack of nonverbals. Of course, sometimes distance is a given, and in this case, technology such as FaceTime or Skype may be the best you can do. Any image of the other side is going to help you communicate better.

Negotiation over screens also can work to your benefit. When the connection gets a little choppy, I try to use those moments to mentally review what has happened so far, digest the data, and figure out my next move. Don't ever panic in situations like this; use them to your advantage. A break in the connection can create a space for regrouping and analyzing what you have learned. I work very hard to take advantage of the pauses that occur intentionally or by chance in the course of a negotiation, and I believe that technology is important to master and understand because our screens are ways that we filter ourselves, our messages, and our character. By the time you read this book, there may be more ways to meet and do business with people around the world. In anticipation of our connections becoming clearer and faster, I believe even more in the timeless practicality of Embracing the Pause (even if and when it gets shorter!).

Bottom line: Beware of technology moving you faster than you want to go in a negotiation. Take advantage of pauses when they occur and build in others to enhance your successful negotiations.

CHANGING THE FOCUS

One simple way to build a pause is to change the subject. I did this at the antique store when I bought the print and flower arrangement for my mom. For a stretch as we shopped, we didn't pay any attention to those items. We looked at everything else, and that helped us keep the other side—the guys who owned the place—relaxed and not expecting anything from us.

TRUSTING THE PAUSE

There is downtime in every type of negotiation, much as there is in nature. When you plant a seed, it needs time to germinate and grow, and it's the same with doing business. Because I am an optimist, I assume that the seeds I plant are growing, not getting killed by weeds or dying a natural death. Setting the Stage and Finding Common Ground have been my trusted ways to make sure those relationships are growing. Yet the reality is that my clients can fire me at any time, so occasionally, when one of them pauses, that can signal unhappiness. The data don't lie: there are many more agents than there are sports professionals who need agents, and so I'm not one to stick my head in the sand.

When I catch myself getting uncertain during the pauses, I remind myself of times when waiting paid off even when I didn't realize I was waiting.

Earlier, I told you about Tom Izzo, the legendary basketball coach at Michigan State who has won the national championship and more than a dozen national coach of the year awards. He's from Michigan and went to college in Michigan before coaching at one of the state's flagship universities. Because I'm from Michigan too and captained the tennis team at Michigan State, Izzo was an even bigger star to me than he would be to people outside the state. As a young agent getting my start in the business, representing someone like Izzo appeared to be a really big stretch, almost impossible.

Starting out, I knew that I needed to tap into my roots as much as possible, and that opportunity surfaced after I received a distinguished alumni award from Michigan State. The local paper reached out to me to write a feature—local athlete making good in the field of sports agency. Since Izzo was on my hot list, I thought maybe he would see it. When the story was published, it was a win-win. The reporter got a good story—very few women were representing athletes, coaches, or sports broadcasters—and I had some local buzz.

I had no idea that after the article was published that Izzo's sister-in-law cut it out and put it on his desk with a note: "If you ever get an agent, you need to get this one." There was a pause between that time and the time when I finally did get in front of Izzo and work out the terms of representing him.

The pauses didn't stop at that first meeting or the next or the next. He was very hesitant to have an agent because he had never had someone work for him on his behalf. Hesitation equals more pauses. He did need someone to represent him to the athletic director at Michigan State as well as to other big universities that showed an interest in him for their vacancies and to NBA teams. Even though Izzo has remained at Michigan State, he often gains the attention of both college and NBA teams in need of a head coach. Our shared Michigan roots became entwined once he realized the value I could add and my enthusiasm for helping him succeed.

This story helps me remember that deals take time, as do authentic relationships that lead to ongoing business. Patience is necessary to endure the pauses. From enduring, you can learn to embrace and use this downtime to your maximum advantage.

PRACTICING THE PAUSE

Precise practice is what you need to improve as a negotiator (or in any endeavor, I believe). Learning to Embrace the Pause is a great tool for building leverage in relationships, not just in negotiating. It opens up and represents the greater possibility for targeted, strategic nonverbal messages.

But how do you begin to recognize the moments when silence is literally golden? How do you learn to step back when those moments occur?

Here is one way to practice Embracing the Pause.

In your next meeting, make a note to yourself that says "Embrace the Pause." Key it into a phone alarm or e-mail notification if need be. Most of us aren't thinking about this, and so much swirls through the mind before a meeting that you need to find a way to incorporate this into your consciousness. You may need to program a 15-minute and a 5-minute reminder as well. It should be your last thought before the meeting begins.

After the meeting, take a few minutes—yes, pause—to reflect on the meeting:

> Were there times when you paused?
>
> How did that feel?
>
> What happened during the pause?
>
> What happened after the pause?
>
> What information did you gain from the pause?

This simple exercise is adapted from mindfulness research, in which neuroscience is used to train people in new patterns of behavior.

The more you repeat exercises like this, the more they will become part of your natural flow for each interaction. As you focus on building your appreciation for the power of silence, you will begin to amass more information that will help your negotiations. As others fill the gap, you will benefit.

You can't make a big ask and expect to automatically Embrace the Pause. Most of us will fill that space without thinking. You have to train yourself, your brain, in a new pattern that will make negotiating more effective. Mindfulness can be a powerful tool.

BACK TO THE FRANCOEUR PAUSE

In the opening anecdote, I left you in bed with Fred and me, listening to the silence. Here's how the whole conversation went down.

When I answered the phone, Frank Wren spoke first.

"You still in the same spot?" he asked.

"Yes, Frank."

"This is incredible," he said, and I could hear the annoyance growing with every syllable. "Just incredible."

He was silent, and so was I. It was like a stare-off, only with a phone in between us.

I put myself in the mental upper deck during that time. I imagined that Wren felt slightly over a barrel because he didn't want to be seen as not being able to come to terms with the young, dashing local hero.

I reminded myself that Jeff's popularity and desire to come to terms didn't obligate me to say anything. I reminded myself that if I did talk, it might give the Braves ammunition against me. There wasn't anything else to discuss; the ask was final.

A full 90 seconds went by, maybe the longest 90 seconds in my life outside of giving birth to twins.

Wren finally spoke.

"Fine. Done. We have a deal," he said. "I'll e-mail you the term sheet now."

Ballplayers like their sleep, but I called Francoeur anyway. I was so excited to tell him that we had gotten him exactly what he wanted.

As much work as we had done in Setting the Stage, Finding Common Ground, and Asking with Confidence, all of that would have been for nothing if we had not been open to Embracing the Pause.

The pause did the work for us.

SUMMARY

A stalemate is a natural part of the ebb and flow of negotiation, and learning to embrace these pauses is essential and strategic. Stopping can open a chance for reflection, create anticipation, remove distracting emotions, shift control, and signal poise. The most important time to Embrace the Pause is after Asking with Confidence.

Master Embracing the Pause by practicing the following habits:

- **Dial back urgency.** Very rarely does everything happen all at once in negotiations. A quick response early on helps build relationships and indicates attentiveness, but after the ask, urgency should be dialed back. It can send the wrong message—that you are rushed, anxious, or desperate.

- **Don't fill space.** Talking too much is a red flag that can signal lack of confidence, nervousness, and discomfort. Embracing the pause projects confidence.

- **Create anticipation.** A pause is an opportunity to create anticipation and consider possibilities. Anticipation creates efficiency, limits errors, and decreases surprises in negotiation.

- **Be patient.** Pauses will occur throughout negotiation, and the heaviest questions may draw the longest pauses. Be patient. The way the other side handles that heavy question tells you what you can do for it.

- **Avoid arrogance.** Be careful that your pause is not construed as withholding information or being manipulative. By projecting a respectful confidence, you demonstrate comfort with yourself and what you have asked for.

- **Sit in the upper deck.** A pause should create enough distance for you to remove any undue emotion that could influence negotiation. You should be able to see more factually and less personally as if you were sitting far from the field of play.

- **Avoid the technology shield.** Technology can move you faster than you want to go in a negotiation. Slow down and seek face time. The more there is at stake, the more you risk by negotiating without getting to read the other side in person.

- **Trust the pause.** Multiple pauses are a natural part of negotiation. Be patient and remember that deals take time.

- **Practice the pause.** Practice simple mindfulness exercises until you're relaxed, and clear thinking becomes part of your natural flow. Practice the pause in lower-stakes negotiations to build your confidence for the bigger deals.

5

Knowing When to Leave

For two years I chased Atlanta Braves star center fielder Andruw Jones. Andruw was a beast, an incredibly talented player who made a splash in the major leagues when as a rookie he hit two home runs in his first World Series game. He was the youngest player ever to homer in the playoffs. Ever since he was a child in the Caribbean nation of Curaçao, Andruw seemed to carry a lucky star around; things always seemed to go his way. He was the sort of gifted athlete who made even the impossible plays look easy.

I wasn't deterred by the fact that Jones had an agent: Scott Boras, a celebrity in his own right, known for his brash personality and ability to nail gigantic contracts for his clients, who have included Alex Rodriguez, Carlos Beltrán, Jason Varitek, and Kevin Millwood. My firm's clients included several big names on the Braves, and I aimed to add Andruw Jones to that list. Everyone knew his contract was about to expire, and his performance had been so dominant that he would be positioned to Ask with Confidence for a significant salary from the Braves or another team.

For two years I showed up when he was in the batting cage. I arranged a private plane to take his wife, Nicole, to the All-Star

Game when he was playing. Other times, I accompanied her to jewelry shows that she didn't want to attend alone. I brought Andruw appearances, speaking engagements, and endorsements.

I dived into this relationship as if I were already representing Andruw. In building the biggest Favor Column you could imagine, I had invested a ton of time and money with no guarantee that it would pay off.

Finally, it was time to get clarity on where all this was going. We booked a private room at TPC Sugarloaf, a golf resort in Atlanta's northern suburbs where the Joneses had built a 25,000-square-foot mansion. We met at their home, where I had been dozens of times. Both Andruw and Nicole had given me tours, and I felt I was as close to family as I could be at that point.

This time I put a bottle of Opus One wine on their kitchen counter. Another favor—at $150 a bottle, a big one.

"Thanks so much," Andruw said graciously.

At dinner were my colleague, me, and the Joneses. Finally the conversation turned to what we were really there for. We Asked with Confidence, because we had been acting as if we had his business already.

"We would love to make this official so we can handle your needs moving forward," I said to Andruw. "We want to talk about how best to manage your expectations of us as we represent you."

Andruw barely paused.

"Yeah, you know I appreciate it," he said. "But my agent—he was there when I got off the boat from Curaçao, and I can't leave him."

That effectively ended our recruitment effort. His loyalty to his agent could not be chipped away by any number of favors or by acting as if we had him as a client. All that investment—poof, gone.

As with Billy Donovan, the coach who changed his mind after signing with the Magic, we were left picking up some very large pieces. What I ultimately learned from this crushing disappointment was how to better assess my chances for a successful negotiation.

Andruw Jones taught me a lesson in Knowing When to Leave.

Ideally, negotiation is a process respected by both sides. Each makes every effort to reach a mutually beneficial arrangement. One of the most difficult aspects of negotiation is knowing when to stay at the table and when to walk away. An obvious mistake that many negotiators make is to ignore the fact that walking away is even possible.

Negotiation can be messy, and so understanding what you are willing to give up and what you aren't is critical. You always want to consider the breadth of possibilities and then narrow that menu to the ones that are acceptable to you. Leaving should always be on that menu.

The title of this chapter could have been "Knowing How to Choose" because leaving is just one choice—the most drastic one. At this point, if you have Set the Stage, Found Common Ground, Asked with Confidence, and Embraced the Pause, you have had ample opportunity and tools to establish multiple choices. With choice, there is a greater sense of control.

You might walk away to pursue an alternative or backup plan that is a better solution than what's on the table. You might walk away because the other party is unable to fulfill your interests. Or he or she might be exhibiting questionable behaviors.

A successful negotiation will end with a result that is better than your best alternative; if you are willing to settle for less than that, that's what you most likely will get. If you are aiming for the best yes, there are signs to look for and tools you can use at this point in the negotiation to determine when and how to extricate yourself.

WALKING AS A PAUSE

Walking away doesn't have to be permanent. It can be a matter of removing yourself from the negotiation with the option of returning at a later time. In this scenario, walking away functions as a long pause. It can be very effective for negotiations that still offer some possibility of closure.

By creating a longer temporary distance, you open yourself to more space and time; both of those elements can foster greater creativity in problem solving. I've hit the pause button on general managers during a conversation, on salespeople at car dealerships, and even on clients while negotiating my own compensation. Pausing gives you a chance to reboot. It makes the other side think and wonder while maybe helping you get clear. Don't be surprised if you walk away with the option of returning and end up with an even better deal.

THE ROLE OF EMOTION IN THIS STAGE

The closer the negotiations get to completion, the more emotion can build up or present itself. This may be because the stakes are high; it can result from the desire to get it done. If a clock is ticking, there may be rising anxiety or adrenaline.

I can't say enough about the importance of staying aware of the emotional temperature in a negotiation and remaining steady and dialed back. You are much more likely to leverage the emotion of the other side if you do not ratchet up when it does. Remain passionate, confident, and enthusiastic but always remain focused on what you have asked for and what you will accept. Continue using empathy as an authentic way to collect information about the other side.

Emotion can keep you in a less than optimal position longer than you intend to be. I know this personally.

GOING TO BAT FOR A TEAM

The closer you are to a situation emotionally, the more difficult negotiating may be. Like most young professionals, I got my start working for someone else. I was grateful to have my ideal job at age 24.

Over the years, I worked for the firm owner. I recruited a team of agents, who were all men. Most were former professional athletes; some were former clients whose pro sports careers had ended, as most do, after a few years (brief compared with nonsports careers). Our firm's network was growing through the personal relationships that each of these agents had brought from his sports career. I valued, cared about, and put my implicit trust in each one of these guys. When they needed something from up the food chain, I acted as their agent with top management.

What they most needed was clarity about the compensation structure. It was ironic that we were known for achieving great clarity in our negotiations on behalf of our clients because internally that value didn't hold. There was no compensation structure.

My history and emotion didn't equip me well for the task of representing my guys. I trusted the system as I rose through it because it remained my dream job. I was good at it: we had signed 300 clients over a span of 15 years, a scale that we had achieved through the growth of my team of agents, who were working 24/7 to sign high-profile talent. I made sure my team knew how much they were appreciated for adding such great talent and numbers to the firm's roster of clients. My salary and bonuses had felt fair to me, and so I thought that must be true across the board. When I realized that my team's success hinged on its members getting clarity on compensation, I went to the owner.

The emotion ratcheted up from there. The owner had started the firm from the ground up. He had leveraged everything to start it and keep it going. He had reinvested his profits in it to ensure its growth. In many ways, the firm *was* the owner. "Trust me" was his message to me and, through me, to my team. To keep my team motivated, I tried to implement bonus structures, but they were hollow measures with "outs." His position remained an emotional one, holding onto what was his and expecting us to feel and act as if we were in his debt. At the core, we had a philosophical disconnect about how to treat employees who work hard and contribute to the firm's success. And how to protect us if the firm was sold. I was unsuccessful in negotiating for a more fair compensation structure and realized that there was no room for a mutually satisfying resolution.

This was not an easy departure for me. The firm had been like a family that had nurtured my career, and I had in turn mentored many younger people to success. But this philosophical disconnect was too great. I left, and so did most of my team. What I took from this was that one of my most powerful emotions—gratitude—could also create blinders, making me oblivious to the firm's disregard for and disservice to those who worked for me. This experience helped me build my antenna for anticipating when to leave sooner so that less is lost. The main symptom that I watch for is emotion, especially swings of emotion such as what I saw in the firm owner and at times in myself. Because his identity was locked into the firm's DNA and I had such intense loyalty to the firm and my team, in our negotiations we couldn't find common ground amid all the emotion.

What that chapter of my professional life also taught me was to work harder on ensuring that there is clarity for all parties.

That was something we always did on behalf of our clients, but we hadn't been so diligent about doing it for ourselves. I also learned the great influence of emotion and pride in a negotiation. I became more aware of these kinds of disconnects, and as I moved into owning my own firm and negotiating more on my own behalf, my greater ability to identify and eliminate these disconnects resulted in healthier and more productive relationships and teams.

THE LEVERAGE OF EMOTION

John Smoltz is a case study in how passion can bleed over into negotiation, revealing information that can make a major difference in whether you can be successful with your ask. It's also an example of how an aspect of your talent and identity can work against you when you negotiate.

Smoltz is an incredibly passionate athlete and person whose long baseball career and success were fueled by his deep well of desire to play. He was incredibly consistent; you could bank on him to deliver on and off the field. Our typical drill when I served as his agent went like this: we had something to eat on his way to the field, and I always brought him the same thing: a cold Diet Coke, a turkey sandwich, and something sweet such as a chocolate chip cookie.

I could always count on his delivery of a blond joke. "I got a new one, Mol," he'd say, and I knew what was coming. It was all in fun, because he was like a big brother to me. We are both from Michigan and huge fans of the Michigan State Spartans. I could also count on John to focus on what we were talking about. We would usually sit on the couches in a stadium office, and his phone would ring constantly. If he didn't ignore it, he would quickly tell each caller, "Can I call you right back? I'm with Molly." It was easy to tell from John's consistent behavior what was important to him and what made him happy.

Everyone knew that about John because everyone had watched him over time and also because John likes to talk and be in the community. He is a huge supporter of a long list of important causes, including the Atlanta Community Food Bank, the Police Athletic League, his family foundation, and a bunch of charitable projects for the Braves. The passion that he had to be one of modern baseball's most resilient pitchers carried over to his work off the field: he had earned the Roberto Clemente Award and the Branch Rickey Award, both for community service. The "Smoltzie" you saw on the field was the same guy who cared so much about what was happening off the field.

Where this emotion did not serve him well was in negotiations. When he was a free agent, every team from the New York Yankees to the Detroit Tigers was eager to lock him up. But every team had the same issue about a deal with him: "Will you leave Atlanta?" It was hard to imagine him doing that after seeing him play only for the Braves and because he was the face of the team in the community. Could he play for another team?

We worked hard to persuade teams that the answer was yes, because he wanted to test the market. It wasn't duplicitous of us to market him as wanting to leave Atlanta, because he had told us he would consider it. But would he actually do it? Even we were not sure. We knew John as a pretty hyper guy who had never changed his mind about playing in Atlanta before this, but he was capable of some mood swings. We also knew what fans knew to be true: John loved Atlanta and felt intense loyalty to the manager, Bobby Cox.

It took a lot of work on our part, but finally the New York Yankees, the richest franchise in baseball, were willing to pay John $53 million to pitch for them. "At least pinstripes are vertical—that'll help you look thinner," I joked with John. I saw this offer as a test of what he felt was most important. Was it the money? His environment? Family? Charitable passions in Atlanta? Golf course options? He was going to walk away from the Yankees or walk away from everything he knew in Atlanta.

The Braves meanwhile saw John as a special representative for them, but at the core, the team's offer of $30 million was strictly a business decision. It wasn't emotional to them. If dollars were a measure of their love, they could not love John as much as he loved them. All the way up the Braves' chain, up to the stoic general manager John Schuerholz, you would see the same facial expressions: This is just business, John. "This is what we can do," they all said.

In hindsight, I see how the team Set the Stage with John. It observed how he was different from fellow pitchers Tom Glavine and Greg Maddux, whose ties to Atlanta were strong but not as deep. They read John's quotes in the paper about how important manager Bobby Cox was to him. When John talked off the cuff during the team's flights to away games or in the clubhouse, that was all data that told them how dug in John was in Atlanta. From that data, they determined that $30 million was their number and all they really had to do was not leave.

Negotiation is like gambling: before you walk up to the table, you must be clear about what your limits are. In the emotion of the moment, the limits will be much harder, sometimes impossible, to determine or execute on. Although I am not a gambler and dislike any form of gambling, I understand the mindset of those who are successful. They have divorced themselves from emotion and read the cues of others to make the decision to leave or stay. Like athletes, some gamblers probably have inborn skills, but mostly they have learned over time what the most important cues are and what their limits are. For them, walking away is always an option, and it has nothing to do with emotion. A team like the Braves knows how to gamble wisely.

The Braves bet that John would ultimately come to them, and they were right. John had spoken to other great Braves pitchers such as Tom Glavine, who told him that other cities weren't like Atlanta, that playing for other managers was a big grind. No one had a player's back like Bobby. John's relationship with Bobby was more important to him than the Yankees' money. Dollars weren't enough to disconnect him from the emotion that went deeper than his profession. His relationship with Bobby was wrapped up in who he was as a baseball player, and his sense of loyalty was strengthened by walking away from the Yankees' big offer. In the end, he accepted a contract extension that made him between $12 million and $14 million a year based on performance.

John is also a dreamer, and his vision, for example, has helped build a wonderful Christian school near his home. He accepted the $30 million feeling that he could build enough favor with the Braves to win the salary negotiations the next time. He felt that the team would owe him, but that was a mistake, because a team is not like a friend; in a year, all kinds of kids come up the farm system who are throwing harder, and the team is looking among them to find the next John Smoltz.

All this had become very personal to John, and frustrating as well. When the next contract negotiation came up, there was no reward from the Braves. The team didn't budge, and that was when John's frustration pushed him to join the Boston Red Sox. The emotion that fueled him as a great pitcher worked against him in negotiation. Passion often doesn't count as much as facts and figures. Emotion can and will be used against you.

Here's a little story within John's story that shows how he used our emotion to yank our chain. He's a big practical joker, and as we flew to Boston in early 2009 to complete the Red Sox contract, he knew we had just gone through the fiasco with Billy Donovan reneging on the deal with the Orlando Magic. "I can't do this," John said to me when we landed in Boston. "I don't want this. Tell the pilot to turn around and go back to Atlanta."

I looked at him, furious. I wasn't in the mood for his joking after everything we had been through. It wasn't just John, of course. As much as I advise clients to detach from negotiations, to not take anything personally and put emotions aside, it's one of the hardest things for them to achieve. And when it surfaces at this late stage, it's beyond aggravating.

"You know what, dude? Just save it!" I snapped at John with a bit of a grin.

He immediately broke into a huge smile. "Just kidding!" he said. That was him being my big brother as usual.

Ultimately, negotiating is the pursuit of change, and every step before the close of a deal involves the careful consideration of what the change will look like. As you assess the cues from the other side, remember that emotion often dictates when to leave because it reminds us who we are and who we want to be.

This sense of identity is probably the biggest factor in negotiation, because it drives why we are negotiating in the first place. If you can get to why, you are in a position to be more successful in negotiating and become more aware of when it's time to pull out.

THE HERO WHO LEAVES

In the situation with Andruw Jones, we found out after two years that we could never occupy the place in his story that was held by his longtime agent. Although he could accept our favors, Andruw could not negotiate with us to become his agent because to him that would have been an act of betrayal. Understanding these values and motivations is the key to successful negotiating.

All of us who negotiate want to be heroes. We want to bring home the biggest catch; we want to nail down the primary resource that will help us and our tribe go forward. We want to outwit our opponents and return unscathed. In short, we are driven by a desire to succeed and become stronger. Or we are driven by a fear of failure or weakness, afraid we are falling behind. Or both. Our species evolved the fight or flight instinct. We learned to read cues about whom we can trust in order to survive. We operate much more on the level of feelings and intuition than on that of facts to make the decision to stay or leave.

If you think of a negotiation as a story that is unfolding, a deft negotiator will establish the common ground that is most likely to provide the setting for mutual success so that both sides return home as heroes. They are building a story together that allows both of them to say that they battled well and with respect. The confidence to ask and the confidence to pause are both signals that we associate with an ally, not an opponent. Still, our human nature puts us always on guard.

Leaving a negotiation means sidetracking the story that you have created because there is a better story to pursue. You or the other side will leave if there is a chance to be a bigger hero by doing so. It's not a question of ego but of self-preservation. Even if the negotiation is in our self-interest, leaving it may be even more beneficial.

RETURN TO WHY

When I wrote about Asking with Confidence, I described the precision involved. You have asked with clarity about who, what, where, and when—this is data. There may even be details about how this gets delivered.

It is at this stage in negotiation that you need to return to why. I talked about this element and its importance in Chapter 1. Deciding to stay or leave often hinges on the reason for the deal in the first place and assessing if those motivations have changed or have been affirmed. Are you still clear on your why? How about the why of the other side? This is another way of circling back to, and ideally reinforcing, the information that you gathered when you Set the Stage and Found Common Ground.

"Why?" is a question that leads to clarity, and clarity helps us to connect with others and ultimately get the deal done or leave with the relationship intact. Clarity in negotiation and beyond guides what we say yes or no to. It allows us to be intentional about where we spend our time and energy when it comes to relationships, responsibilities, and negotiations. Saying no, which is basically the message you send when you leave, can be difficult. Sometimes we have a tendency to drain our energy by investing in the wrong things and the wrong people, and asking why at any stage of negotiation can help you see if that bad investment is happening. Clarity makes it easier to act with intention.

When I think of clarity, I picture summers spent on the lake in Michigan, looking through the clear water to the very bottom. The rocks lie on the lake floor 20 feet below, but the water is so pristine that you can see the rocks despite the depth. Clarity allows you to see deep down. I think of the rocks as the foundations in life— career, family, and faith for me and whatever those foundations may be for you. As negotiations approach the end, an agreement, a compromise, a temporary pause, or a point where you walk away, these rocks should become clearer to you. Sometimes it's tough to sort out what these things are to you and to the other side, but with practice you will see more clearly. Start by asking yourself why more often. Outside of negotiating, this habit can help you be or become more intentional about the priorities in your life, which will carry over into negotiations. It will also help you define what success in each of those areas of life looks like to you.

ACTIONS AND INSTINCT

Another key habit to develop in this stage of negotiations is to become hyperaware of actions. Don't be surprised if the other side can and will say anything to keep you in the deal. What you want to weigh more heavily are the actions that you see. If the other side's actions contradict its words, its actions will always be a more accurate indicator of its intentions.

Precedent can play a huge role at this stage as well. Knowing the tone, tendencies, past behaviors—any history of the other side—will help you know when you have reached the limit with it.

Even more accurate is your own instinct. In *Blink*, Malcolm Gladwell describes the human brain's ability to "thin slice" vast quantities of data and messages to determine the key factors that are most important to making a good decision. That observation leads to the suggestion that we should trust our gut to tell us what the best next move is.

DON'T MAKE ASSUMPTIONS

In the case of Andruw Jones, two years had gone by without my asking a simple, broad, powerful question:

"Why do you like your agent?"

Maybe I thought it was too obvious, or perhaps I assumed that because he was taking deals and was appreciative of our support, that equaled opportunity for us. In the end, it came back to haunt me because if I had asked, I know Jones would have said that Boras was his first ally in a new culture. Boras was his lifeline.

If I had heard that—and because I have heard that sort of comment from so many other athletes who come from other countries—I would have immediately recognized who Boras was to Andruw: a father figure.

I would have known that Andruw was locked in to Boras. That one sentence would have told me that their relationship wasn't in Andruw's eyes built on a foundation of business. It was about devotion.

I determined that I needed to dissect future relationships on the front end by looking for cues and asking the right questions so that I could head off this kind of fiasco before it happened. Dissecting it after the fact wasn't going to help. I needed to be ahead of the other side so that I would Know When to Leave.

I began to listen for the differences between statements and stories. A statement might be, "Oh, we love our agent." It is an opinion that exists apart from any deeper relationship. There is no narrative, no beginning, middle, and end. Statements are highly negotiable.

A story is much deeper and more persistent, and it represents the core of someone's identity. "Oh, he was the guy who met me off the boat from Curaçao" is the story of an ally who is critical to Andruw if he wants to become a hero. When he does deliver at the World Series, Boras is part of the legend. There's a beginning, middle, and end to Andruw's baseball story, and Boras is a main character in it. Without Boras, Andruw wouldn't have become the Andruw who accepted the Opus One and all the other favors and then said, "No thanks."

When I think of being locked in with an athlete, coach, or broadcaster, I am an integral part of their story. They can't see their future without me in it, because I have been such an important player in their past and present. Although I work hard to get to this point with every client and recruit, it's even more important to understand what it looks like to the other side.

For Andruw, Boras was the first guy he saw when he got to the United States. He believed in Andruw's talent, took Andruw under his wing, and represented security. As strong as Andruw was when I met him, Boras had seen him at his most vulnerable, and that was where their relationship had been cemented. Why did I miss seeing this in the two years I chased Andruw? My assumptions mattered more to me than really finding out his story.

I learned that the Favor Column, Finding Common Ground, and Asking with Confidence would be in vain if I did not pay attention to the other side's stories. These stories are worth learning and could save you years of fruitless efforts.

LEARNING FROM WALKING AWAY

Walking away from a deal is hard. You may feel failure, or relief, or other deep emotions. Negotiation is difficult, immersive work that drains the mind, heart, and spirit. I've learned to look back for important lessons.

Chasing Andruw Jones helped me see the bigger picture of what my firm wanted from a relationship with him. I had been so focused on representing him as a client that signing him was the endgame. For my firm, clients were the bricks that were building a strong foundation of marketing to corporations. With a stable of star athletes, coaches, and broadcasters, another level of negotiations would be open to us to represent those stars to big businesses that wanted to sponsor them or set up partnerships to promote their work. One negotiation led to another, because one relationship led to another. Because my side of the business was recruiting, I had been less aware of what my success meant.

As I paid more attention, I saw new opportunities in that world for my abilities. A vast and exciting world, beyond being a sports agent, where my expertise, personal story, and experiences would be even more valuable. From this awareness, I have built my present platform in the broader world of business. After spending almost two decades as a sports agent, in 2010 I decided to start my own company. I saw many parallels between the sports space and the business world, and that led to an opportunity to share my experiences with a broader audience. I spend a large amount of my time traveling the country speaking to Fortune 500 and other corporate audiences about business development, leadership, teamwork, and recruiting. Our company is all about transforming the relationships that make business successful. We do a lot of team development work as well both with companies and with sports teams. Would I have moved into this new sphere without chasing Andruw Jones for two years? Yes. The point is that when negotiations fall apart and we walk away, our natural reaction is to maintain forward motion to get us away from the damage. We don't want to associate ourselves with something that didn't pan out or, even worse, blew up. Set aside that inclination and take the time to look back and look around. Even more important, look inside. Taking stock at this point can inform everything that happens going forward. I guarantee that a hard look at what went down when you walked away—or when the other side walked away—will benefit you in the long run.

THE UPSIDE OF NO DEAL

The Andruw Jones experience numbed me. I couldn't believe that someone would take and take with no intention to give back.

And I learned plenty myself. The Favor Column meant nothing to him ultimately. It didn't mean I would ditch the Favor Column; I still saw its power for me, but I learned that it wasn't always going to hold power for others. My eyes were wide open to the realization that anyone is capable of taking favors without any intention of giving back. That is why the giving must come from an authentic place. Giving can be strategic, but it must be authentic. From that new space of understanding, I was better equipped to recruit and sign Jeff Francoeur. I needed to have the guts to ask the harder questions sooner. There would be no more years of chasing and making assumptions, no matter how big the prize.

As you assess the other side in the later stages of negotiating, it's always beneficial to play out the repercussions of every possible move. Although my goal in a negotiation is to Ask with Confidence and close a deal that is mutually beneficial, obviously, not every deal works out. What I do have control over is my view of the situation and the forethought I bring to the outcome, no matter what it is. I am rarely taken off guard, and even in the most difficult negotiation breakdowns I always find pieces of wisdom and important relationships that are worth preserving. This doesn't just happen; you need to value resilience and act with integrity and confidence throughout negotiations. Only then will you consistently mine negotiations for your greatest business and personal success.

KNOWING WHAT YOU GIVE UP BY STAYING

As an agent, I am not the person who says yes or no but the advisor to a client who is going to pull the trigger or walk away. Knowing When to Leave can become clearer when you understand what you give up by staying.

In the mid-2000s, Franklin Langham was on the verge of breaking into the top echelon of PGA Tour players. By qualifying for the Masters in 2001, he had boosted his visibility and marketability. He became the target of several equipment manufacturers. They compete to sign up the most players, betting that some will become superstars and that fans will want their clubs, bag, hat, apparel, and golf balls. The industry is not locked up like sports programming, which is dominated by ESPN. The PGA Tour is a collection of independent contractors who negotiate for themselves. In some ways, it's a little like horse racing or the stock market: equipment manufacturers and corporate sponsors invest varying amounts in players, depending on the likelihood of each one getting hot or staying on top.

Among equipment manufacturers, Titleist always had the most players signed to play its golf balls. When Nike came out with a ball, it approached us to see if Franklin would sign with it. It wanted to make the swoosh as prevalent in golf as it had become in basketball and running. Just as in many businesses, the money is dangled before those who switch, not those who stay. Our position was that if Franklin felt good about the ball, the money was significant, but we would never advocate for him to change the core resources that had gotten him to the top. His real fortune would be realized by staying at the top of his profession, and that was our foremost goal. This is always the difficult decision: to turn down a deal that may not be there the next year. These guys live on an edge made up of many variables, and they base decisions on their capacity for risk and confidence in themselves. Franklin was a thoughtful guy who knew that money was not the solution to everything in life. He had a college degree (in risk management and insurance, which prepared him well for his business decisions) and plenty of support at home.

As it turned out, Nike's money was enough for Franklin to switch from Titleist. Nike agreed to pay him between three and four times what he had received from Titleist. Unlike Nick Cassini, Franklin handled the ball switch well. We left stacks of Nike balls in the locker room for Franklin, and he took advantage of off days to hit the new balls on the range. Because he was emotionally and mentally ready to switch a part of his game that he had to trust implicitly—and because he owned the decision to switch—the Nike deal was a great decision for him.

The next season, Cleveland Golf was taking the PGA Tour by storm with its driver. Franklin had struck gold with the ball deal; now he was considering giving up the club with which he hit off the tee. The risk was just as big, maybe bigger. In golf, as in most sports, it is hard to pinpoint one variable that will cause an athlete to burst into the limelight or drop into a slump. A new ball or driver will get the credit or the blame because people want to be able to identify a definitive reason for an athlete's performance.

The new driver didn't work the same magic as the Nike ball. It was a disaster. Franklin had been known as a steady driver of the ball off the tee; with the Cleveland club, sometimes he was hitting it sideways. But he couldn't switch back because he was under contract with Cleveland. The inconsistent driving began to affect other parts of his game too, and he began to drop down the money list.

What Franklin's story tells me is that it's important to be very clear about what you are passing up when you stick with what you have. Franklin would have missed out on a great deal on a Nike ball and all the money that went with it. He also would have missed out on a not so great deal on a Cleveland driver and all the money (and heartache) that went with it. Past performance often indicates future performance, but not always. The assessment and understanding of capacity for risk is most important so that you can leave or stay with confidence.

Franklin and I remain friends today because in our negotiations as agent and client we had clarity. He knew that we owned the terms of the deals with his equipment companies and that we put our reputation behind what we offered him. We knew that he owned the risk of getting locked into gear that might not be a great fit. This is important to note because negotiations are not always going to look great in hindsight: I wished he hadn't signed with Cleveland, and so did he, but we went forward together. In negotiations, transparency and clarity work together to create trust and solidify the long-term relationships on which great businesses are built.

BEWARE OF FEAR FREEZING EITHER SIDE

Continuing to move in negotiations takes energy that you might take for granted if you are used to a fast pace of business. You may not even recognize the inertia that must be overcome to continue to negotiate. Only when discussions grind to a halt do you realize how hard it is to get going again. As the moment approaches when a decision must be made and, preferably, you have some sort of deadline to drive your deal, fear is most likely to enter the atmosphere and cause havoc.

This fear is real. I think of athletes such as Brian McCann, a boyhood friend of Jeff Francoeur, who through hard work forged a major league career that eclipsed even Francoeur's. McCann was also from the Atlanta suburbs—his heart will always be in Atlanta—but he had the fearlessness to recognize that emotion and the haters among the team's fan base who would feel betrayed, move past it, and accept an opportunity to play catcher for the New York Yankees for $85 million for five years. When you see a big deal like that inked, you must realize that both sides came to an understanding that they could get beyond fear and the idea of walking away and continued moving toward a contract that both believe will be mutually beneficial. It's easy for the average sports fan to shrug and say that for that money, of course he would leave, but it's never that simple. The dollar figures, performance clauses, and other elements of a successful salary contract are a window into the story of both sides and their tolerance for risk and pressure.

Regardless of whether you leave a negotiation or maintain forward momentum, the best deals are made with your eyes wide open and a clear understanding of the new world that is being created by the two sides. As someone once told me, "The grass might be greener, but you still have to mow it." This statement is a great reality check, especially in high-stakes deals.

If your gut tells you that the greener grass is going to be too hard to mow or not worth mowing after all, it's time to leave.

SUMMARY

One of the most difficult aspects of negotiation is knowing when to stay at the table and when to walk away. A simple mistake many negotiators make is to forget that walking away is even an option. Withdrawing from a negotiation should happen only after one has weighed all the factors carefully.

In making that decision, use the following parameters:

- **Dial back emotion.** The closer a negotiation is to completion, the more emotion can build up. Emotion can and will be used against you if you don't remain steady.

- **Gamble wisely.** Before you walk up to the table, be clear on what your limits are. Study cues from trustworthy participants in the negotiation. Step back to see your chances of success better.

- **Return to your why.** Gain clarity around why you are negotiating. This will help you figure out if, when, and how to leave.

- **Actions speak louder than words.** At this stage, the other side may say anything to keep you in the deal. Actions are always a more accurate indicator of intentions.

- **Don't assume.** Learn the difference between statements and stories. Statements are negotiable; stories rarely are. Assumptions often overshadow the real story.

- **What if I stay?** Understand what you give up by staying. It's important to be clear about what you are passing up when you stick with what you have.

- **Fear paralyzes.** Fear usually enters the picture when a decision is imminent or a deadline is looming. You need to be prepared to soothe the other side's trepidation and stay authentic and steady. The best deals happen with your eyes wide open.

- **It's not always permanent.** You can still leave open the option of returning to the table. The space and time created by walking away can foster greater creativity in problem solving.

- **Look back.** When negotiations fall apart, our instinct is to avoid looking back on the wreckage. Look back and look inside. A failed negotiation can be the best teacher of how to succeed in the next one.

The Power of Gender

It's almost dinnertime, and as I hurry out of the office, I am grateful that my commute home takes only five minutes. On this night, ESPN broadcaster Erin Andrews and a girlfriend are coming over to hang out with my family. My daughters love Erin.

As she is showing them some moves from her days with the University of Florida's Gators Dazzlers basketball dance team, my phone rings. It's an endorsement deal I had been working on for her. I break from the fun to step into my home office to work out some of the details for a women's health product. The deal will involve a daylong appearance, a production day, and the rights to Erin's name and likeness throughout the country for 12 months.

"Come on, girls, you can do it!" I hear Erin in the background, cheering on my girls. My negotiation call has ended, and I'm back in a line dance with them. It's so much fun, and Erin is right. We can do it.

In business, negotiations are still dominated by men. The more successful you are in an industry like sports, the fewer women you see at the table. The scene at my house that night, with women anchoring almost every step of the deal, is unfortunately all too rare. But female involvement in negotiating is only going to increase, and it will be a curve you do not want to be behind.

DOES IT MATTER?

Yes, the more women see the opportunities in negotiating, the more they will seize the opportunities, and that will benefit us all. How does that affect you if you are a guy reading this? You are living with, working with, or selling to women, and that proximity means you are negotiating with women whose decisions influence your life. Understanding the unique factors that inform our decisions is an awareness that you should be cultivating.

According to a 2013 Nielsen report, women in the United States control two-thirds of the consumer wealth that keeps the economy going, and women negotiate differently. "Women remember more and differently than men do, so talk to both her emotional and rational sides and acknowledge her attention to detail," Nielsen recommends. "Layering emotional decision-making opportunities with rational information will increase purchase intent and will have strong 'sticking' power. According to Nielsen NeuroFocus, the female brain is programmed to maintain social harmony, so messaging should be positive and not focus on negative comparisons or associations."

Gender in negotiations is important because of the disconnect between our economic and personal assets, our values, and the way we go to bat for what we need and want. In short, gender is powerful because either overtly or subtly it can limit what we think we are allowed to ask for—and whether we ask at all.

Every step that I have examined so far—Setting the Stage, Finding Common Ground, Asking with Confidence, Embracing the

Pause, and Knowing When to Leave—is the same for any negotiator, male or female. But gender is an aspect that is difficult to escape in negotiations and must be managed. This chapter points out what research and my experiences reveal about how gender may be influencing you as a negotiator in each of those five stages. My goal is for you to accept gender as one powerful aspect of negotiation and make it work for you, not against you.

FINDING COMMON GROUND

As the general manager of the Atlanta Braves, John Schuerholz was almost a generation older than I. That alone could have intimidated me, but what was most in play the first time I walked into his office to negotiate John Smoltz's contract wasn't age. It was gender.

John was a free agent and was being courted by other clubs. As his Atlanta-based agents, we arranged to connect with Schuerholz in person. Our meeting was in Schuerholz's office at Turner Field, where the Braves played and John pitched.

Schuerholz speaks fast. He is abrupt, smart, and savvy. After shaking my hand, he pointed to his desk: a perfect rectangle, tidy, with two chairs in front of it.

"Sit down. Right there, perfect," he said in a clipped millisecond.

He turned and spoke only to my colleague. I realized that Schuerholz thought I was a secretary, present only to take notes for my male superior.

I needed to establish my presence and authority in a firm, friendly way. I had to keep it authentic.

My eyes wandered to the screen saver on the computer behind him, where images of various famous golf holes rotated in quick succession. I recognized the beautiful par-three twelfth hole at

Augusta National, where the Masters is played every spring only a couple of hours from Atlanta. It's a prestigious course where at the time no women were members. Playing there was by invitation only.

The small talk between my colleague and Schuerholz continued into the third rotation of the screen saver. When the twelfth hole popped up again on the screen, I took my chance.

"Did you play Augusta?" I asked casually.

Schuerholz nodded.

"What did you get on number twelve?"

He perked up immediately and seemed proud to discuss it or surprised I knew what hole it was. Probably both.

"I parred it," he said, and our first connection was made.

"Nice," I responded. "Great hole." I softened my voice and facial features. "I actually birdied it last week."

The next 10 minutes were occupied by one topic: golf. Midway through, I felt that I was in Schuerholz's inner circle. He knew me not as a person who didn't make a difference but as someone who shared his love of golf and had experienced a place that he and the world view as prestigious. This earned me instant respect.

Would the same thing have happened if I were male? Perhaps. But my intuition told me that his initial disregard for my presence had to do with my gender. I felt this at times in my profession because so few women were present. Even today, not much has changed. Schuerholz and powerful people like him never had to learn to view women as negotiators because they had never seen a woman in that role. As I rose in my profession, I saw no women across the negotiating table.

We live in an era in which those preconceptions are fading, but not quickly enough. As I write this, fewer than two dozen Fortune

500 CEOs are female. No matter how those statistics evolve, I believe that gendered differences will always influence negotiations.

WHAT THE GAP LOOKS LIKE

This gender gap in negotiating and the unfortunate price women pay for it are well documented. The 2003 book *Women Don't Ask: Negotiation and the Gender Divide,* based on research by Carnegie Mellon economics professor Linda Babcock, argued that this gap is costly for companies because women are getting only what they ask for, which is not as much as men request.

"Observing these inequities, women become disenchanted. . . . When a better offer comes along, rather than using that offer as a negotiating tool, women may take it and quit," Babcock reports. "This happens even in organizations that make concerted efforts to treat women fairly. . . . They do not realize that the men are asking for a lot more than the women are."

In more recent research into male and female negotiation patterns, cultural influences persist. "We do have a greater expectation of niceness from women than from men," says Hannah Riley Bowles, a professor of public policy at the John F. Kennedy School of Government at Harvard University. "There's a body of research showing that when women step into the realm of stereotypically masculine behavior and need to use an authoritative or directive leadership style, or need to aggressively claim, 'You should give me more money and resources,' that this doesn't feel right coming from a woman. There's some research that shows there's a backlash to women stepping into these masculine roles."

Writing for Forbes.com in a feature on the tenth anniversary of the publication of *Women Don't Ask,* conflict resolution expert Victoria Pynchon echoed this reality. "Not only has our culture instilled in women a disinclination to be self-serving, when we do work up the nerve to ask, we're likely to experience 'gender blow-back'—a subtle but powerful punishment for stepping outside our cultural gender role. . . . Women suffer economically because we fail to ask, but we're punished for our nerve when we do ask. We're damned if we do and damned if we don't."

In a negotiation, you get what you expect of yourself as a man or woman regardless of what you have asked for. Men are getting more pay and compensation because they expect it, and more of them are more practiced in asking for it, which means more of them are more confident and more successful.

Meanwhile, women fulfill expectations set by others that they will accept less pay, and they accept less because they don't expect—and Ask with Confidence for—more.

KNOWLEDGE IS POWER

One barrier that I've observed for many women is that negotiation appears complicated and scary because it's messy and uncertain. The effort and resources that go into it are not guaranteed to produce a favorable result. Relative to men, women are new to the world of corporate business, and a conservative approach is more appealing to most of us. We don't see women making the ask, much less Asking with Confidence, so we don't see ourselves doing it. Not negotiating brings more of a sure result than does negotiating.

Research shows that when women know how much they should be making—from a pay scale that is set—they negotiate and accept pay at a rate that is much closer to that of their male counterparts. It's when the compensation becomes more blurry, such as with bonuses or allowances for moving expenses, that women are more likely to accept less. When there are no standards for a negotiated agreement, gender is more likely to come into play. When women don't know what to expect—when they "don't know what they don't know"—they end up accepting less than a man would.

One survey showed that men are four times more likely to negotiate salary than women are. When women do take that leap, they ask for less. When they succeed at getting a raise, it is 30 percent less than the raise for a man in the same position. Whereas men report higher levels of fear of losing a job offer by negotiating (36 percent report this fear compared with 29 percent of women), significantly more women than men say they lack negotiating skills (26 percent versus 18 percent). What this pattern says to me is that women need to double down on Setting the Stage to get the most accurate comps they can for negotiating a complete compensation package equal to their worth in the market. They may need to work on Finding Common Ground with the gatekeepers of that information. Women negotiate best when they know the bargaining range and appropriate standards for agreement. In such a scenario, gender triggers are far less likely to influence either side.

"Once we get a handle on . . . what a willing buyer would pay a willing seller, gender notwithstanding, we can begin to have a conversation leading to agreement," said Pynchon, an attorney and commercial arbitrator, in Forbes.com. "That's all a negotiation is: a conversation between two or more people whose purpose is to agree to terms beneficial for all. The good news for women is that we love conversation. We're also pretty fond of agreement."

INCLINED TO BENEFIT OTHERS

What these data and my personal experience reveal to me is that women are more likely to lack confidence and less likely to look for opportunities to negotiate. It's hard to say which came first, but the mindset and the inner reserves work together for any successful negotiator. Confidence or the lack thereof can be a male or female trait. So is the mindset that anything is negotiable. So why isn't it?

When I walked into the orthodontist's office to discuss my daughters' need for braces, I could Ask with Confidence because I had researched the anxiety points that the orthodontist typically faces. This preparation was the main reason she was open and accepted my offer to prepay for services at a 33 percent discount. I also had trust that was based on my referral from a dentist she knew. Perhaps the fact that we were both women didn't matter. However, my gut tells me that she was more inclined to accept a creative, mutually beneficial solution from a fellow female professional who knew what she was up against.

Research shows that women exceed men in negotiating on behalf of others, and so we should try to put ourselves in a position to do this as much as possible. "Women outperform men in representational negotiations—that is, negotiating for someone else," says Stanford Graduate School of Business professor Margaret A. Neale. "As a woman, it is unacceptable for me to be greedy on my own, but it's completely acceptable for me to negotiate for someone else, because that is a caretaking thing, a communal thing. I've certainly had women CEOs of moderate-size to large organizations tell me they have no problem negotiating on behalf of their company. But asking the board of directors for a raise? That is hard."

As more women understand this general inclination, I believe more will step up and find a comfortable spot at the negotiating table. Why shouldn't we excel? We juggle and improvise all the time to make ends meet. We fill our needs and those of our bosses, coworkers, and family members just as our mothers and grandmothers did inside and outside the home. Juggling is just another name for negotiating. If you are successful at getting needs met across an array of factors, you are a successful negotiator.

VALUING DIFFERENCES AND CREATIVE SOLUTIONS

By valuing these daily life experiences more and seeing ourselves as the skilled negotiators we are within the domestic and personal spheres of life, we can bring a unique perspective to business negotiations. I have seen too often that male negotiators think of a finite number of options. They are inclined to an "I win, you lose" mentality. They see one pie that can be split only in certain ways. Because I naturally juggle and seek options for balance, I am quicker to see trade-offs that create value, to see beyond the edge of that pie plate. The whole concept of a Favor Column is about creating value instead of engaging in direct competition. This is one way that I've embraced and worked with gender expectations in a male-dominated industry.

I have tried to understand those assumptions and use them to my advantage. If our culture pegs me as a peacemaker, I'm going to use that for everything I can to bring about a healthy result in my negotiation. In this way I am copying the great coaches and athletes I have been privileged to watch and represent. They don't fight their assets and weaknesses. They work to make them a package that is stronger than the sum of their parts.

This strategy would fall under what Harvard Business School professor Kathleen L. McGinn, an expert in negotiation and a noted researcher, calls reducing gender triggers. "There are situations in which you can reposition the bargaining in a way that is not gendered," she says. "For example, if I see an opportunity for leadership, and believe that in that position of leadership I can attain additional value for those who would be working with me, then I can face the negotiation not as grabbing everything for myself but rather as an opportunity to increase the value for a whole bunch of people. That tends to demasculinize the situation."

HUNGRY GIRLS AND AN EMPTY POCKET

I'm on the way to soccer practice with my girls, and we've got to grab a quick dinner. We pull into the drive-through at Chick-fil-A, and I realize that though I've brought my driver's license, my wallet is back home. Everyone's hungry, but what can I do?

Negotiate. I know Chick-fil-A prides itself on being family-oriented and that its employees have more power than most to make choices like this. Plus I have a communal concern: my children are hungry.

"This is so embarrassing. You are not going to believe this," I tell the guy at the counter. "But can I ask you if I can pay you tomorrow? I come here three times a week, and my wallet's back at home. I promise, promise, promise I will come back and pay you."

"Yeah, no problem," he replies. "We know you." I got his name and rolled through the drive through the next day and handed him cash. He just smiled as if to confirm that giving and trusting a good customer works.

Some people might say that asking like this takes guts. What we should be asking is: Why don't more women do it? What makes us afraid to ask for what we need or want? Why is it harder for women than for men to negotiate?

"People, especially women, need to broaden their definition of what it means to negotiate," Stanford's Margaret Neale says, adding,

"It's your job to think: 'Is there a creative way for me to engage my counterparty in a way that I am better off and he or she is at least as well off?'"

I couldn't agree more.

LEARNING FROM PRO TENNIS

In the wake of Sheryl Sandberg's book *Lean In*, *Sports Illustrated* looked at gender differences in the likelihood of a pro tennis player challenging a referee's call.

Male and female players have three challenges per set, and a recent study showed that women consistently challenged far less than men did (2.6 percent of points played at Wimbledon in 2013 compared with 3.3 percent for men during that event). That means men players challenged 25 percent more often. It makes a difference strategically, because the success rate for a challenge is almost the same across genders. So why don't women pro tennis players question authority as a way to negotiate on the court? I like what tennis legend Martina Navratilova said: "As women we need to be more comfortable challenging. Here's one area where there's no reason we shouldn't be just like the men."

Note also that the tennis pros had no idea this was happening until the data were presented to them. This is another example of why it's important to dig deep when you Set the Stage and go beyond conventional wisdom to see how gender and less visible factors may be influencing the other side in your negotiations.

SETTING THE STAGE

When we talk about comps, research has shown that men can have a view different from that of women. There are data suggesting that men are more likely to take a desired action if they know that a high percentage of their peers have taken that action. Women are more swayed by a comparison to actual people they know. Hiring managers use these types of data to negotiate differently with prospective employees on the basis of their gender.

"You might tell a male prospective hire that you're offering him more than you'll give others with his qualifications, assuming that is true," said the professors who authored the Harvard study "Men, Women, and Status in Negotiations." "When negotiating with a female prospect, you might be more specific: 'We recently interviewed someone similar to you. . . . To signal how much we want you to work for us, we're offering you more than we offered her.'"

Even if you disagree with this strategy or find it offensive, it's important to know that gender differences in negotiating are real and are being manipulated all the time. The higher the stakes are, the more time you will want to spend Setting the Stage. Gathering information about gender as it relates to the other side—and deciding how to build a strategy with or around it—should be part of your process. You have to assume it is part of the other side's.

SEEING THE OTHER SIDE THROUGH A FAMILY LENS

Earlier, I talked about a deal for Mark DeRosa, his grateful brother, and the power of using the word *you*. After that deal with DeRo, I began to see negotiations through a different lens that ultimately helped me make better asks. You might call this my communal lens, to use a term popular among academic researchers. Seeing how these brothers had each other's backs made me think more about how our family ties influence negotiations. How does what I do as a negotiator, what I ask for and settle for, ripple into the lives of others?

The more I considered this, the more powerful this idea became, and the more it influenced the way I negotiated. I began to see how everyone involved with each negotiation has a mother, a father, and often a brother or sister too. Our families often teach us our first lessons in negotiation, including whether to stand up for our needs or wants. All these lessons affect our present negotiation.

With this knowledge, I began to pay even closer attention to anything those on the other side said about their families. This information held more weight for me in terms of Setting the Stage and Finding Common Ground. Family stories offered clues to personal and professional histories of getting what members of the other side want and need in life.

I'm not getting into Freudian psychology here, I'm just saying that you can take a lot of intimidation out of negotiation if you think this way. It's a version of "the other guy puts on his pants the same way you do," but it adds a layer of compassion and intimacy that can work in favor of a more successful outcome. Studies show that women negotiate better when they see connections like this. Also, when you see yourself as an equal to the other side, as just another person with a unique backstory that includes family relationships, you feel more balanced as a negotiator. It's much easier to feel confident, and confidence is what many women struggle with.

The DeRosas helped me see how our language and family history shape the way we ask and how comfortable we feel doing so. Remember, it's just a conversation.

STEREOTYPING IN NEGOTIATING

I have spent a career being instantly set apart on the basis of my appearance. This can work for or against me in my professional and personal life.

Consider what happened when I went car shopping. I knew that whoever wanted to sell me a car would bring all of his or her experiences and expectations to our negotiations. By Setting the Stage, I was aware of these factors. When the salesperson asked me, "What do you do?" I tested a stereotype.

"I'm a kindergarten teacher," I said. I knew that this answer would fit what the person probably expected in my answer. It's easy to believe that a smiling blond woman could play the role of a kindergarten teacher rather than that of a sports agent. That stereotyping changed the negotiations for the car, because the image of a teacher is sympathetic because she is underpaid, especially compared with a sports agent.

The point I'm making is that stereotypes are important to understand so that you can use them to work for you and not against you. There's little point in arguing whether they are right or wrong. They exist—and they are powerful. I advocate transparency in deal making partly because women can't hide their gender.

Stereotypes are cues for what others expect that we will do and what we should do. As research shows, if we buy into the way others stereotype us, we are sacrificing our worth. Too often we have had to choose between being nice and getting what we want or need because we perceive a much higher risk in asking than a man would see. We need more women demonstrating and practicing a negotiating style that is both nice and assertive, both warm and expectant. I believe strongly that this is possible because I have seen it work over and over again in my male-dominated industry.

The bottom line is that if you're not aware of gender stereotypes and issues in negotiating, you are neglecting a vital factor that can make or break a deal.

PRACTICING A NEW PERSPECTIVE

Some days, all day long, I work as a facilitator between service people, my business, and my family. Fathers and mothers all over the world play the same role. We problem solve to our greatest advantage and, most often I think, to the benefit of our communities.

When you begin to understand how much you negotiate already, you can see that almost anything is negotiable. Maybe not the price you pay for gas at a convenience store but many services and costs. As you become better at negotiating, you will gain self-empowerment.

Often this translates to greater status in a group. Because people, especially women, do not like to negotiate, those who do this well (or at least don't mind trying) have an asset that can help them negotiate with the group. Almost every student fund-raiser, for instance, needs sponsors. Using the steps in this book, I can knock out several quick deals with local businesses to secure sponsorships or donations. It's fairly easy and routine for me to build a Favor Column this way among the parents who are involved with these projects. A big bonus is that my volunteer work gives them a sense of how I do business, and they may reach out to become clients.

This mindset will also circle back to Asking with Confidence. As you find more opportunities for negotiating, you can practice more. The more you practice, the more skilled you will become in Asking with Confidence. Practice is particularly important for women because it demonstrates that we aren't accepting our limitations. Many of us have bought into the illusion that negotiating skill is something that we lack because we weren't born with it.

Heidi Grant Halvorson, a psychologist who has studied gender differences in career success, described this pattern in *Psychology Today*: "Because bright girls are particularly likely to see their abilities as innate and unchangeable, they grow up to be women who are far too hard on themselves—women who will prematurely conclude that they don't have what it takes to succeed in a particular arena." For too many women, that arena is negotiating, but it's not too late to change that. As Halvorson says, "When it comes to mastering any skill, your experience, effort, and persistence matter a lot." That comes down to one little word: *practice*.

LOW STAKES, HIGH RETURN

A fundamental aspect of Asking with Confidence is practice, and this is paramount for women in particular. Practice negotiating when the stakes are low so that you will think more quickly and better when there is more on the line.

Recently I spent two hours with Kathy Betty, one of the first female partners at Ernst & Young, and we talked about women and negotiating. We spoke about achieving a comfort level in negotiating through repeated practice. Only through practice does anyone make something difficult look easy. Practicing negotiation can put you face-to-face with gender bias (internal and external) and force you to deal with it. That's the only way this culture truly will shift—by women acting differently to challenge those perceptions.

"It is often expectations, attitudes and values that follow behavior, rather than the opposite," notes Harvard public policy professor Hannah Riley Bowles, who has studied challenges for women leaders in negotiating. Her prescription, as I see it and agree with it, is to first see ourselves as capable negotiators. Then we can feel more deserving and expectant of success. We won't be treated or allow ourselves to be treated as deserving less when we negotiate.

Here's some good news and fuel for those of you reading with reluctance: "Our studies found that women respond immediately and powerfully to [negotiating advice from a manager] and rapidly begin to see the world as a much more negotiable place," Linda Babcock reported in "Women Don't Ask: Negotiation and the Gender Divide."

I agree with many of the sentiments in Sandberg's bestseller *Lean In: Women, Work, and the Will to Lead*, which states that women have all the hardware needed to compete in business, including negotiation skills. It's our software that needs work. We need to reprogram the way we think of ourselves, especially our capacity for risk and for going after what will make our lives and the world a better place.

When we avoid negotiating, when we don't hold our own when we do ask, and when we sell short our abilities, we add to what Sandberg calls the "ambition gap," where our desire for approval keeps us from ascending to leadership roles. We can't rise fully if we don't feel comfortable negotiating.

COMFORT WITH UNCERTAINTY

Another way to build confidence is to reframe your success in terms of negotiating well. You may not be appreciating the obvious in your experience and therefore may be missing the chance to translate and leverage that experience in the arena of negotiating. For example, working moms, especially those in the corporate world, may not give themselves credit for the key negotiations that they've already handled in combining a career with a family.

Social scientists would say you are already a "two-level job negotiator," and firms such as Deloitte & Touche have found greater success in recruiting and retaining executives once these women (and men) are empowered to manage their careers and professional lives through a customized schedule, pace, and work-load. What Deloitte is fostering and valuing—which is so smart in this era—is the skill of creating personal balance. By tapping into the way professionals negotiate in their personal lives, the company makes employees feel valued. By Finding Common Ground, the company has Asked with Confidence, and its employees have responded. If other companies aren't trying to copy this model of "mass career customization," they should be. It is a great example of the power of changing negotiations by changing the underlying assumption that work should look the same for everyone who is on a career track.

Research has shown that women with fulfilling careers and personal lives have adjusted their mindset. They understand that having both spheres of their lives operating well means giving up some expectations. If everything is important, nothing can move forward; negotiating is about that give-and-take. I like what the authors of *The Orange Line: A Woman's Guide to Integrating Career, Family and Life* discovered when they researched how 118 success-ful career women managed the complexities of work, family, and personal life.

Those women, the authors found, shared responsibility for home and family—they were not the only ones carrying that load. They no longer felt that they had to be perfect in everything. They told themselves they were good enough, they expected to be paid for the full worth of their skills and contributions, and they took responsibility for their own growth. These assumptions in effect Set the Stage for positive negotiations on behalf of themselves, their families, their employers, and their clients.

PERMISSION TO NEGOTIATE

Most important in my opinion was that this population of successful women *stopped seeking permission to negotiate.*

"Everyone tells women to negotiate more and so many women don't. Research has found, however, that when women have permission, they do negotiate—and often out-negotiate men," Forbes.com writer Kathy Caprino noted. "For example, if a job has been advertised that 'salary is negotiable,' three times as many women will apply for the posting than they do when there's no mention that wages are negotiable. When women believe they are invited to negotiate, they do so much more readily than when they fear they will be seen as 'pushy' or 'demanding' to get what they want."

This holds true in what I have seen in my career: when it comes to negotiations, women are more likely to be passive. Their reluctance to negotiate (and, when they negotiate, to negotiate in a mediocre manner) is why, for instance, male managers consistently have higher starting pay than women do. You cannot achieve your full growth if you don't negotiate. Wait for an invitation to negotiate and you will be stuck. Meanwhile, others who are more comfortable with making the ask but are not necessarily more talented get ahead.

If you need any more convincing about the gender gap in negotiating, there's evidence from the federal government. Some elected officials are trying to address our disparity in compensation through a proposed law called the Paycheck Fairness Act.

It would prohibit discrimination in pay based on gender, and it is designed to keep that from continuing. One measure it includes is authorizing federal grants for educational programs to train women and girls to negotiate for equal pay better. I'm not saying that more government is the answer, just that this provides even more evidence that differences between men and women's skills in negotiating are significant, documented, and pervasive.

ASSUMING AUTHORITY

When we talk about negotiating being messy, we're talking about the many gray areas that come up and that must be hammered out so that both sides feel listened to, understood, and honored. How do you feel confident doing that without experience? And how do you get experience without being confident?

I believe one way women can feel more empowered is through what I call assumed authority. You may have heard this described as "act as if." This is the thinking behind the Favor Column. You are serving a person as a client even before that person has agreed to a formal relationship. You are assuming the authority to do so. This leap is particularly useful for women who may lack experience—and a comfort level—as negotiators.

We know from sports psychology that your mind cannot tell the difference between real and imagined practice, that when you practice visualizing what you want to see happen, your mind frames that as reality. Because of the way they are socialized, more women than men assume that they don't have authority. This sets up the gender gap in negotiations.

One key to assuming authority is to project warmth and high expectations of others. This combination rings true to my experience as it was described in a recent Harvard Business School project. As one way of addressing the gap between male and female academic performance, the school's female faculty was studied and coached to become stronger teachers. Female professors "who plainly wanted to be liked sometimes failed to assert their authority—say, by not calling out a student who arrived late," the *New York Times* wrote in an article about the project. "But when they were challenged, they turned too tough, responding defensively." Warmth and high expectations were the way to bolster their credibility, and it worked. By the end of the semester, "the teaching scores of the women had improved so much that [the project manager] thought they were a mistake."

Note also what was going on before this change in tone and intent. Not only were the women failing to assert authority, but they were defensive when challenged. The women professors possessed very few gears that would help them go forward. They weren't versatile in their response. Their tools for negotiation were limited. A successful negotiator demonstrates a warm authority and confidence that is most authentic when it is part of that person's perspective on life. You will be most successful in negotiating when you naturally demonstrate the grasp of warm authority, and you can start achieving that with assumed authority.

BABY STEPS TO CONFIDENCE

Here's another personal example of practicing negotiation skills. It's 5 p.m. on a Sunday, the final day of a big soccer tournament that my daughters have played in. Summer is so hot in Georgia that we're ready to pass out. A merchandise trailer is parked near the soccer complex, and the guy inside is getting ready to wrap up after a busy weekend in broiling conditions. He's got a bunch of T-shirts to box up, T-shirts that my three girls want.

The sign says the shirts are $22 each. That's $66. That's a lot of allowance money. And who knows if they'll even wear them after today? I want to help them get a nice souvenir (just as I did for my mom at Callaway Gardens), but I don't want them to spend any more than they have to. The setup appeared to be a one-man operation, which meant the guy doing all the work had the authority to make decisions.

"Sir, you don't want to pack and carry all those back, do you?" I say to him. (I'm Setting the Stage.)

He smiles, tired. "Tell me about it," he says. (We Found Common Ground.)

"Listen, I've got three girls playing here, and I'd love to get one for each of them. Ten for each?" (I Ask with Confidence.)

Pause. (Embraced)

"All right," he says, looking around, wanting to make sure he wasn't giving the deal to anyone else. "Done."

Each of the girls put up $10 of her own money for a shirt. This was the biggest piece for me, teaching them how to negotiate. When you are making a deal, it's usually to benefit a wider circle of people than just you. Thinking like that, especially if you are female and feel reluctant, can help you warm to the challenge.

As we made our purchase, some other moms came up and asked about the price. I kept my eyes on the guy who had made the deal with me. "Two shirts for forty-four dollars?" a mom asked him. He looked at me a little sheepishly. My face told him the fair market price was in play for my fellow mom. "Two for twenty," he said to her.

Now, a handful of soccer T-shirts is not going to change the world. But establishing common ground for a worthy cause is where change begins. It's the start of strength that can challenge even the most hardened forces.

VALUING AN APPRECIATION FOR OTHERS

I love the old saying, "Women hold up half the sky." I think sometimes we hold up more than that. As a working mom who is supported by a great husband, I either perform or oversee most of the work needed to make our family operate. This has given me a deep appreciation for the woman on the front line of keeping my household going, our nanny, Dottie.

Finding and negotiating to hire her and to keep her employed with us helped me see how I believe women can use their sensitivity to build a better deal regardless of the gender of those involved. Instead of being overly sensitive to fear—fear of asking, fear of not getting, fear of what other people may think—I believe sensitivity can make us open to a mutually beneficial solution based in deep understanding of and appreciation for one another's gifts. We have the greatest need for turning defensiveness into curiosity and the greatest ability to do so. In my experience, women especially have a tendency to let fears or others' expectations dictate too much. Fear inhibits curiosity and can make us oversensitive to rejection. We have to put our egos aside and have a real love for learning and feedback. Women and men who embrace feedback are receiving a gift and being mindful of that is a big part of growth.

Going into the nanny search, I knew that I was looking for a unique person who could make an unwavering commitment, and this held immense value that I was willing to match with an attractive compensation package of salary and benefits. My oldest daughter was one, and the twins were three months old. My goal was to find someone who could work for us at least until the twins were in kindergarten. I was looking for someone who would almost be a family member. She would be the glue for us, the engine behind my ability to do the work I do in a relaxed way. I don't care if you are Michelle Obama or Sheryl Sandberg; you cannot get on a plane and leave your kids if you don't have someone who is just as strong as you are at home.

With Dottie, our negotiations followed the pattern in this book. I paid a great deal of attention to Setting the Stage to discover what she needed. Finding Common Ground was about the kids and to a certain extent about my budget. I didn't want to overpay her and not be able to keep her for the long term, so I worked hard on determining what an adequate Favor Column would look like. Making the ask was a positive experience for both of us, because I felt so great about our fit together and because we could pay her what she had requested, give her benefits such as vacation time, and build in bonuses that would keep both of us happy in terms of our financial expectations.

This transparency has built an incredibly special relationship that has helped me keep Dottie from getting poached by another family that might be willing to pay her more. I can't afford to let that happen! I have worked hard at keeping an open line of communication with her so that we can talk about anything that is a problem. Although this may sound like a purely personal negotiation, working parents know how incredibly difficult and critical it is to nail down this assistance. You can substitute any important negotiation for this one. For me personally, a deal doesn't get any bigger than this.

Let me leave you with this wish. Women have specialized, amazingly awesome emotional wiring, and we need to value how creative and generous we are and how we are equipped to hammer out complex solutions that benefit multiple stakeholders. When we move toward this understanding, we can create a better world for women *and* men. The whole sky will be much better for it.

SUMMARY

Gender is powerful in negotiation and a factor that both men and women need to be aware of. For women, gender stereotypes and expectations can limit what we think we are allowed to ask for and whether we ask at all. Whether or not we recognize it, gender influences our conversations. As more women see opportunities to advance through negotiation and seize those opportunities, their status in business and as influencers will increase.

Here are some of the elements to be aware of:

- **Specific standards reduce bias.** Gender triggers are far less likely to influence either side when the standards for a negotiated agreement are clear.

- **Frame your ask around the benefit of others.** Research shows that women exceed men in negotiating on behalf of others. Harnessing your heart and mental savvy makes for the best ask no matter what your gender is.

- **Value creativity.** Women are more likely than men to see past a finite number of options.

- **Find your communal lens.** Women negotiate better when they see connections. Recognize that what you do as a negotiator causes a ripple effect in the lives of others.

- **Practice a new perspective.** Many women believe they are not born with the skill set to negotiate. This is self-limiting and can be negated through practice. Look for bias (internal and external) and tackle it through small-scale negotiations. This leads to confidence.

- **Get comfortable with uncertainty.** Negotiating is about give-and-take. Women with fulfilling careers and personal lives have adjusted their mindset to understand that success is elastic. Not everything happens at once in negotiation or life.

- **Stop seeking permission.** When women believe they are invited to negotiate, they do so much more readily. Recognize that this reluctance to negotiate hinders growth.

- **Assume authority.** Women often are socialized to believe they don't have authority, which is necessary for negotiating. Telegraph authority by projecting warmth and high expectations of others.

- **Build better deals.** Regardless of the gender of those involved, greater sensitivity makes all of us open to a mutually beneficial solution based in understanding and appreciation.

Going Forward

Every April, two nights before the Masters golf tournament begins, about a dozen of us in the business of pro sports get together for dinner near Augusta National. On one of these evenings I found myself in conversation with Butch Harmon, one of the foremost swing coaches in the game and among the top-ranked teachers in the country.

The son of a pro golfer who won the 1948 Masters, Butch had watched several generations of the top players from inside the ropes and was the mechanic for some of the most highly tuned swings in the game.

"Butch, you work with some of the most incredible golfers in the world," I said. "What's different between these guys who are in the top 10 in the world and the rest who are trying to win?"

Butch answered immediately. "Their ability to recover from adversity," he said. "These athletes recover fast."

Butch's authority on this went deep. Not only had he witnessed his players overcoming great odds in competition, but he was in the middle of doing the same thing. Butch had just been fired from coaching Tiger Woods on his swing and was about to start working with Phil Mickelson. At one time or another his stable included Greg Norman, Adam Scott, Davis Love III, Stewart Cink, Justin Leonard, and Ernie Els, among others.

Resilience is one of the key aspects of successful negotiating. In the previous chapters, I've outlined the elements of every successful negotiation: Setting the Stage, Finding Common Ground, Asking with Confidence, Embracing the Pause, and Knowing When to Leave. In Chapter 6 you read about the power of gender as an influence in negotiating. If you stop reading now, understanding each of these parts will help you negotiate better in the same way that knowing the parts of your car will help you communicate with your mechanic.

Read further and you'll see how all these elements come together and you'll also find my best answers to the most common questions I am asked about negotiating. This chapter will reinforce the idea that every deal is different. Let's be honest: there's never an easy negotiation—that's a contradiction in terms. But you can make it easier on yourself.

Just as the parts of the car depend on a steady supply of gasoline to keep moving, a negotiator needs a source of mental fuel to keep going forward. After watching and learning from great negotiators and nailing big deals and failing at others, I've distilled the most critical personality traits. These traits are the fuel for successful negotiators.

RESILIENCE

The pace of negotiation can be incredibly fast. You have to listen, digest, and make decisions while keeping pace. In this way, negotiation can be like elite sports. In the NBA, the NFL, or any professional team sport, everyone on the playing surface is a superb athlete.

Their fast-twitch muscle fibers are all on alert. They are primed for actions that the rest of us can only dream about executing.

But even more important is their reaction. Sports are dynamic, especially when speed is introduced. The reflexive movement toward the ball or another athlete is what matters. Sure, the guy who can make 100 straight free throws is talented, but he's not a star until he can hit a jump shot at the buzzer to win the game. Then he has delivered when it most counts.

Being resilient is part of having a high degree of self-awareness. You recognize that you are on a downward (or at least not upward) path, and you can turn things around. Resilience is making a choice to take the high road in an unimportant tiff with your spouse instead of digging in and creating a bigger mess. It's letting go of the past, even if the past is one minute ago, and starting over by looking forward. I'm not suggesting forgetting the past, because it's all important data. Just don't get stuck in what has happened.

When I think about Butch's comment, I realize that the top golfers especially develop short-term selective memory. As independent contractors, they have only themselves to rely on when a round starts to go south. A great golfer such as Tiger Woods knows that he chooses the story that he will tell himself just as surely as he chooses what club and shot to use. Resilience is the understanding that there are always choices, and choice always gives you a sense of control. That's what you want when you negotiate, because there are so many variables—so much messiness—that it's easy to feel out of control. Resilience helps you realize that ambiguity is a natural part of negotiating and that you can be just fine not knowing exactly where you stand. There are times when you don't say what you mean or wish you could take back what you did say, and this is when resilience helps you forgive yourself and move forward with the conversation.

OPENNESS

Phone calls at 2 a.m. have not been uncommon in my world, especially when my clients are performing on the other side of the country and wait until after the game to call me. But one call from the other side of the world sticks with me.

The excited voice on the other end of this 2 a.m. call was not familiar. Brent Abernathy was a talented second-round draft pick from Atlanta who had flown to Australia to play winter baseball (it's sunny Down Under at that time of year). Brent knew that as his agent, I was going to pick up the phone any time of day or night.

"Oh, my gosh, Molly, I just won a bunch of money!" he said, almost breathless. He had been in a casino, playing poker, when he was dealt a royal flush. The hand earned him six figures, something like $120,000—more money than he had ever had at one time.

I knew he must have been pinching himself—was this really happening? I also heard an edge of fear in his voice. "What do I do?" he wanted to know.

My fatigue had quickly given way to adrenaline. He was fired up, so naturally I was too, but I dialed back.

"You want to get it in the bank, right?" I asked him. "Because if you do, we need to get you to transfer it back here to a bank and help you line up a financial advisor."

"Yeah, I think I'll keep five hundred dollars," he decided, sounding relieved. "But other than that, I'm going to wire it back."

A couple of years later, Brent's major league career was over almost before it started. He had a brief cup of coffee with the Minnesota Twins. The casino winnings and that story were part of his baseball history. (So was Brent's schooling me on the difference between a glove and a mitt and never referring to spikes as cleats. I needed that!)

The 2 a.m. phone call left me with several levels of the same message: you never know. You never know when your phone rings who will be on the other end. You never know if the cards will be a decent hand or duds or crazy good like Brent's. You never know if all that talent is going to take hold and last or fizzle.

Brent's phone call stands out to me as a reminder to always stay open. Expect the unexpected. This is so important in negotiating, to maintain a mindset of openness to anything happening. Openness is the wide lens beyond what I can see in the moment and the knowledge that there is a lot that I don't know.

Without openness, you can't have 360-Degree Awareness. With openness, you understand that every action is planting a seed for something else to happen now or in the future. This was especially true in the Detroit deals that I described in Chapter 2, "Finding Common Ground." My initial deal with the water and Mike Maroth gave me an in that led to other negotiations with other players and businesses.

Openness helps me remember to respect the person who appears to be in the way of my forward movement and success. I've seen situations in which that person will walk into the room one day and take a seat across the table. You never know when your paths will cross and where you might meet again. The Golden Rule applies to negotiating, big time.

VISION

The U.S. basketball team in the 1996 Olympics, like the one four years earlier, was loaded with so many great players that people called it the Dream Team. Its coach, Lenny Wilkens (a Hall of Famer as the NBA coach with the most wins), was our client. We got Lenny a $200,000 endorsement deal involving a few appearances and a commercial for BellSouth Mobility.

A few days after inking that deal, we received a call from BellSouth, the parent company, which wanted to be associated with the Olympics. As we put together a $300,000 deal for Bell-South, we were amazed at the disconnection between the two parts of the same company. By probing more deeply, we realized that this was happening at a lot of big companies: as the business of sports boomed, they were scrambling to get in on the action, and their efforts were scattershot. We realized that we could go beyond representing talented athletes, coaches, and broadcast-ers. We branched out to represent companies that wanted in on sports marketing.

BellSouth gave us a very healthy retainer to help its multiple brands create a more holistic approach to big sports events and make the most of that investment. We showed the company where its dollars would make the greatest difference for consumers and business clients. We couldn't have done this without the two deals related to the Olympics, because those deals helped build trust across the BellSouth entities. The companies were comfortable with us because we had delivered to each of them in a timely and professional manner.

In retrospect, the way the first negotiations led to the retainer seems like common sense. But on the front end—where we were seeking to work out a deal—the best solution for both parties wasn't crystal clear.

This is where vision comes in.

Vision wasn't just observing that BellSouth Mobility and its par-ent, BellSouth, weren't communicating. We could have stopped there and patted ourselves on the back for two deals that made us more money than a single one could have. We had the intelligence to take that unusual sequence and ask what message the market was sending. The key was looking beyond the first and even the second deal to see a whole new field with many other (and more lucrative) negotiations.

Vision is also the understanding that each negotiation carries the seed of the next one. You may be dealing with the same party or the same type of ask again.

More likely, it's more subtle than that. It might be a relationship that is formed or deepened through the negotiation, and most likely it will be the knowledge that changes you. Even when you fail at a negotiation, you have gained wisdom that will help you succeed in a future deal.

I am an optimist by nature, and I have a glass-half-full mentality. My years of doing this have taught me that if you don't pick up whatever pieces can be salvaged in every negotiation, you won't be in this business very long, and for the time you are in it, you won't be very good at it.

Lenny Wilkens's career is a study in the power of vision. In high school, when players work hard to get the attention of great college coaches, Wilkens didn't think he was good enough to play for his school team in Brooklyn, and so he competed in youth leagues. He didn't see himself as being at the level of his peers. He ended up playing for Providence and making All-American, but even when he was picked in the first round of the 1960 NBA draft, he wasn't sure he wanted to sign because he had never seen a pro game. Once he saw the level of play among NBA guards, he decided he was good enough. So began a Hall of Fame career of more than 40 years.

Bottom line: once Wilkens could see himself and his competition clearly, he knew what he needed and wanted to do. Success at his level doesn't just happen. It takes vision.

A big reason I preach 360-Degree Awareness is that it promotes vision. You can't be aware of what is possible without vision.

With it, you can see your way out of even the toughest jam. Vision keeps you moving because you can see where you're going.

SEEK WHAT'S GOOD

My oldest daughter gets in the car fresh off a soccer practice. "Steve is mean," she says unequivocally about her coach. "He got so frustrated when we didn't do a couple of moves right and started yelling at us."

Five minutes later, we're picking up her sister, my younger daughter, who's walking toward me in her gymnastics leotard with a big smile and beads of sweat dripping down the side of her face. Before I can even start the car and ask how practice went, she is brimming over with emotion.

"Mommy, I love Jane—you know, the new coach?"

"That's great," I tell her. "Tell me, what do you love about her?"

"She's happy, Mommy. You can tell she wants to be there, and she really wants me to do well."

The contrast between the two coaches' styles hit me square between the eyes. Steve is overwhelmed by seeing errors among young kids; with children in virtually the same age group, Jane is overjoyed to see their great potential.

You might recognize yourself as more of a mean Steve than a joyful Jane or somewhere on the continuum. In negotiation, it is important to seek what is good because it opens your mind to possibilities that you may not see. Potential is what negotiation is about; it's another word for what could be created between two sides. Be careful not to get bogged down by what you see in front of you, especially missteps and screwups that are part of the messiness of negotiation. Absorb all of it as important information while you seek the good.

DISCIPLINE

The pitcher stands alone on the mound, peering at his catcher's signals before delivering the pitch. The ball sails across the plate, just missing the outside corner. Ball four. The batter trots to first base. The pitcher wipes the sweat from his brow and walks deliberately to the back of the mound. He grabs the rosin bag and turns to face the next batter. He approaches it as if it were the first pitch of the game.

She tosses the ball high and slams a serve over the net, but it skids wildly away from the line—a double fault. She puts the racquet in her opposite hand, takes a deep breath, and nods at the ball boy. She selects the ball, and this time she nails it: an ace down the center of the court that catches her opponent off guard.

What trait do both of these athletes exemplify? Discipline. It's the mental discipline that makes these athletes successful on top of all the physical discipline that you must have to get to a competitive level. They have disciplined themselves to accept errors as part of the game and not be undone by them. The discipline to take setbacks in stride allows them to succeed. The loser is the one who can't stop the downward slide. Discipline helps pave the way to a quick rebound.

This subject came up on a recent flight with my 10-year-old daughter.

"What is discipline?" I ask her, thinking she might say it's something her parents do to her as punishment.

"It means to prove that you can do something that you thought you couldn't do but you actually can," she says matter-of-factly.

I'm glad she thinks of it this way because as we mature, we learn that we have to be disciplined for ourselves. I love this quote from John Wooden: "Discipline yourself and others won't need to."

Negotiation is often a minefield of adversity. The best athletes in the world know what this is like. Sometimes we think athletes must be superhuman. The most successful performers are exceptionally disciplined in their response to adversity. They don't allow it to consume them; instead, they embrace it as a challenge. They create routines that help them recenter and remain focused when otherwise they might start to slip. They root themselves in preparation and trust in their work when the game is on the line. Recovery from adversity takes discipline.

Discipline is intentional. It demands practice. When you become disciplined in the ways you think, these thinking patterns become ingrained habits. This repetition is the force that puts your ideas into action even in adversity. This is driven by the belief that if you follow through on a necessary action—and enough necessary actions—you are in the best position for success. Discipline indicates that you're on a clear road, moving ahead, not all over the map.

With discipline, there is growth and a greater awareness of gaps. You're not going to see where you can add value in one day; you build that by observing every day until you start to see patterns and needs. Discipline involves patience. It's where the rubber meets the road.

ETHICAL COMPASS

Don't make assumptions. Believe the best but be prepared to accept the worst. People are going to take with no intention to give back, as we saw with Andruw Jones. This ties back to resilience because you are going to be dealing with people who may not be living according to the Golden Rule the way you are. The ethical compass indicates when you have been wronged, and it reminds you that you have choices. Most important, own your response.

CREATIVITY/IMPROVISATION

We all feel comfortable when we know what to expect. "I'll have the usual," you tell the barista, who knows your name and serves the coffee just as you like it. But how much of life, much less negotiating, is like this?

It's messy and ambiguous, but creativity turns stress into enjoyment. I see this all the time in sports. Athletes and coaches have practiced the fundamentals for years; they've got all the parts down cold. They try to prepare for every scenario, but it's all just practice until the tip-off, kickoff, or opening drive. When the action starts, that's when all that practice pays off.

One of the greatest shots in golf, at least in recent memory, was the improbable recovery shot that Bubba Watson hit during a playoff at the 2012 Masters tournament. Stuck on pine needles behind a tree, Watson faced 164 yards to the green. He needed a miracle to get on the green, and that miracle could not have happened without the creativity he needed to see the shot he wanted and somehow execute the big bananalike hook. The ball ended up on the green, and two putts later he was the champion—thanks to creativity and improvisation.

In music this is also true. After all the hours of practicing vocals or an instrument just to get the scales, pitch, and delivery right, a musician can improvise to create music unlike anything anyone has heard before. A musician's true voice can be heard in the way he or she adapts during an improvisation.

When you are negotiating, know that every deal is different and every deal is a chance for your unique style of problem solving to shine and improve. Mastery of the fundamentals gives elite performers powerful tools for problem solving in crises. Creativity and improvisation are the means to overcome roadblocks and find a way even when there doesn't seem to be the possibility of forward movement.

Combine what you know in a fresh way. We all have creativity, and with practice we can learn to identify our greatest resources and be great improvisers on our feet. It's fun!

GRATITUDE

A big antidote for the stress of negotiation and the experience of rejection is gratitude. The practice of gratitude helps me stay centered and keep my perspective and focus. It is a go-to tool when I realize I am taking things personally and need to dial back to the facts.

Gratitude forces you to shift your mindset. By pausing to be grateful for the little and the big things in life, you find more mental space for the next action you need to take in negotiation. On my list of things I am grateful for are good health, faith, family, the Midwest values I was raised with, my sense of humor, big brothers who treated me like a little brother when we were growing up, sports and all its emotions and lessons, my team at my company, my speaking platform that allows me to create connections and improve lives . . . and my running shoes.

Gratitude as described above is more of a personal, private practice to help me keep moving forward, but the results are very outward. I know that I project true focus because gratitude helps me stay in balance. Gratitude has a counterintuitive place in negotiation. Authentic thankfulness can make a powerful connection to the other side. Telling people you are sincerely grateful that they listened, that they responded promptly, that they respect you—all this can create a personal connection.

If you are comfortable communicating gratitude in negotiation, I urge you to pair it with a pause. If you immediately follow it with a request, the listener will hear the request and forget your thanks.

If you follow it with "but," you've negated your gratitude completely and risked having your listener feel manipulated or alienated. Let your gratitude show, and your negotiation will benefit from it.

THE MOST COMMON QUESTIONS ABOUT NEGOTIATING

I'd like to take the opportunity to answer the most common questions about negotiating that I am asked when I speak or coach in business settings. I encourage you to ask yourselves the same questions as you grow in your ability to negotiate, because there will be others who come to you to learn your wisdom. Your answers may be different from or build on mine.

Negotiations constantly challenge me to build my base of what I know, whom I know, and how I work with people to understand their needs and targets. It is such a dynamic world that I expect my answers may change, but for now here are my most thoughtful responses.

Who Are the Toughest Types of People to Negotiate With?

Stubborn, closed-minded, unhappy people and those who like to argue more than work toward a solution. I've learned to look for a moment, a crack in the chatter, to ask them simply, "Do you want to get a deal done?" These are the people psychologists call crazy makers, and it's important to set boundaries, speak directly, and hold your ground with them. Otherwise they will drive you crazy and make you feel and act out of control, and often you will end up walking away from something that you really want to make happen. Or you may give away what you want to keep just to make the crazy maker go away. Don't let that happen. Keep breathing,

Embrace the Pause, and if you ultimately decide to walk away, do it after careful consideration of your goals and actions.

Who Are the Easiest Kinds of People to Negotiate With?

Smart, open-minded people who are generally happy, healthy, and productive. Every signal they are sending out is one of benevolence and agreeability. This doesn't mean they'll give in or give away everything. They project an open heart and face to the world and most often are great listeners. They're also honest and keep their word.

The easiest way to find these types of people to negotiate with is to be this type of person yourself. Like attracts like. A positive outcome breeds great memories and feelings. We all want as much of that as we can, and this is how longer relationships are created. When I talk about vision and the seed of each negotiation being planted in the present one, all of this begins with you. You have far more power to set the tone and project the desired outcome than you know.

How Did You Learn How to Negotiate?

By doing it and not being afraid of a no. This is the biggest fear that people have, even people who are supersuccessful at very intense jobs and high-pressure careers. They fear rejection.

What I learned quickly is that a "no" in negotiating doesn't have to be personal. It can be if I choose to make it personal, but rarely do I raise the stakes to that level.

What else can "no" mean? It can mean "maybe," "not now," or "try again." When I hear "no," I try to move quickly from any defensiveness to curiosity. "Tell me more" is how I respond.

You have to stay in the game, continue the conversation, and not let any feelings of rejection stop your momentum. Whenever appropriate, treat a "no" in negotiation more like a yellow light than a red light. This is how you keep negotiating and keep learning how to do it better.

How Do You Negotiate with Someone You Don't Trust?

If you must negotiate with someone you don't trust, you need to build more scaffolding around the deal to make sure that what you're trying to build doesn't fall down. What holds up a deal is trust and respect, and if you are constantly questioning whether the other side is for real—is it really going to do what it says?—it's hard to get the traction you need.

First, you must be everything the other side is not. Don't play games. Keep records of what happened when so that you can refer to facts. You may find it advantageous to keep the conversation more about data and what can be quantified, because numbers, dates, and facts are fixed and irrefutable. Keep your tone, energy level, and response time steady, not high or low. This will give you a greater sense of control and help you project stability. Remember that you are inviting members of the other side into a world that feels safe and comfortable, where their help and contributions are a way of making that world complete.

This is your foundation of respect. You may not respect them yet, but you hope they can trust and respect you. At this point, look for the opportunity (without changing your tone or approach) to probe what's happened so far in the negotiation to see what their experience has been. You want to check in gently to see if they are remaining consistent in their answers and experiences. Give them a chance to build a new record of honesty that you can trust.

Above all, stay close to the information and knowledge that make you authoritative. Remain curious and empathetic. Take your time. If there is any doubt that you can trust them or can trust them enough with what is at stake for you, that is a signal to leave. Don't do a deal if ultimately you cannot establish enough trust.

Are Negotiations Harder When More Money Is Involved?

You would think I would say yes. We are trained to have our eyes pop out when thinking about deals involving sums of cash from six figures on up. A successful negotiator, though, sees that money more in the abstract, as an impersonal object. What more money does is make deals more complex. More people or stages or details are involved, and sometimes that means that more time is needed.

In my experience, though, money is not the deciding factor in what makes negotiations difficult. The game changer always has a face. I am much more concerned about the people I will be negotiating with than about the amounts of money that will be transacted. Those sums are inanimate, tangible blocks of commerce. If you want complicated, study the people who decide how much, to whom, when, how, and where.

How Do You Find a Connection with Someone Who Offers No Initial Connection?

We're all different. I never take it personally when someone with whom I am negotiating seems distant or reserved or less than interested in connecting. There is a certain type of person who likes to hang back and wait for the other side to open up first, kind of like in boxing or poker. I believe these people feel more comfortable being reactive, and they see connecting first as a huge risk. That's important information for me as I go about Setting the Stage.

Being comfortable with not making a first connection is part of being an authentic chameleon. In Chapter 1, I described the importance of this ability to adapt to any situation. If my counterpart in negotiation is introverted or standoffish, I go into dig mode. I don't go overboard, but I do make an extra, relaxed effort to find a professional or personal interest. It may take a little while, but I am determined to establish a zone of safety and comfort around our conversation that will help bridge the disconnect.

However, reluctance in making a connection is more a point of style than a roadblock. You have to make at least some basic connection to negotiate. I believe that we all want to connect. It's in our DNA to want to create something that is left behind after we are gone. We can do that only by connecting. If someone is a bit frosty to me from the get-go, I rise to the challenge and dig to find a link.

How Do You Negotiate with People You Don't Like?

I try hard to minimize the time spent in negotiations like this. I am very outgoing and disposed to like other people, but of course there are people who, for one reason or another, I don't connect with as well as others. That is human nature.

These strong feelings are a signal to look inside myself for why. More than anything, I don't want my personal judgments working against me, causing me to rush the deal or agree to what I don't really want just to get away from a person. Here are some key questions that I ask myself in this situation:

- Am I being fair?

- Can I put aside my dislike for the time being to deal with this person?

- How can I use this challenge to know myself better and become even better at being an authentic chameleon?

I do not advocate being a fake, ever. Study the other side and absorb as much of its world as you can so that you can find the best way forward that complements both your and its goals. This takes much more energy when the person is unlikable. It's important to own those feelings and move through the negotiation as quickly as you can without rushing. Life is short!

How Much Can You Plan Out a Negotiation?

Negotiation is much more about preparation and anticipation than about planning and scripting. This is why so much of what I advocate is about understanding yourself, amassing important information about the other side when you are Setting the Stage, looking for creative ways for Finding Common Ground, and fostering the self-awareness needed to Ask with Confidence. These are guideposts for your journey rather than a map.

I began this book with this thought: negotiation is a conversation, not a script. You would not script out a conversation with a friend, but you might remind yourself to tell that client something important or to make a timely point. When your client brings up something new, you absorb it and ask questions. You expect give-and-take, to both listen and talk, to pause and react to what is said and what is shown. You may not be aware of how spontaneous your conversation is, especially with someone you trust. You may take for granted how quickly you think and how creative you can be in storytelling, changing topics, and displaying humor. Just as a good conversationalist reads social cues, a great negotiator stays aware and avoids impulse moves.

Negotiation demands that you recognize and channel conversation skills. Just as you see topics that you have in common with a client and/or a friend, in a negotiation you must have the ability to see as many options as possible and help the other side see the benefit that you see. One of those options is to step away. Embrace the Pause when you need more space or the other side is preparing a response. Anticipate, be prepared, and have confidence in your tools.

How Did You Get Comfortable Being the Only Woman in Negotiations?

Growing up with two brothers, I never knew any different. The boys always outnumbered me, and if I didn't claim my own ground, I would be left out.

Those odds helped prepare me for my career. I could see that in negotiations I wasn't just the other side, I was the other gender. Just as I did with my brothers, I framed my identity and appearance as a positive. I stood out, yes, so that meant those on the other side might remember me better if I was competing against others for their business. That would gain me only a certain amount of initial attention, though. I needed to deliver quickly the superior level of service that made them feel special, too.

Our differences never stopped me from focusing on what I could do for them. I tried to be consistently courteous and honest, neither pressing nor trying too hard. I had some good mentors too, who helped remind me that a negotiation doesn't have to happen all at once.

SUMMING UP

Let's circle back to where this book began, with the premise that a negotiation is a conversation. While I was writing this book, I had the chance to attend the 2014 Rose Bowl and see my Michigan State Spartans beat Stanford.

When we arrived in California, our hotel rooms at the Ritz-Carlton weren't ready. It was two hours before we could get in. By the time I got the key, the guy at the front desk wanted to make it up to me.

"Here are some discounts at the spa for your inconvenience," he said. The two coupons were worth $10 each, not much of a saving considering how much pedicures cost at the Ritz. Besides, our stay there was going to be busy; there was no time for spa services. The idea he had was positive, but what he gave me might as well have been Monopoly money.

I paused and smiled and then handed him back the coupons.

"Can you send up a bottle of wine?" I asked.

"Done," he said, nodding.

Every day we are going forward in our lives, giving and receiving, *asking for what we need and want* (or not, if fear gets in the way). My fervent hope is that this book equips you to prepare with precision and confidence to negotiate from a place of warmth and transparency. I believe that if you consistently employ the methods I've described in these pages, you will become both a more successful negotiator and one who gets more enjoyment from the process. By learning as much as you can about the other side, you are putting yourself in the most advantageous spot to learn more about yourself as well.

I've mentioned how important stories are in negotiating and business, and I hope you will share your story of better negotiating with me and subscribe to my online newsletter. You can do that at www.mollyfletcher.com. I look forward to keeping our conversation about negotiating going.

Connect with me:

Twitter: @mollyfletcher

Facebook: /fletchermolly

E-mail: molly@mollyfletcher.com

Bibliography

Adelson, Eric. "Billy Donovan Comes of Age." Yahoo! Sports, March 14, 2013. http://sports.yahoo.com/news/ncaab--billy-donovan-comes-of-age-030340735.html.

"Agent Cost Him $2M, but Niners CB Might Get Some Back." *USA Today*, August 20, 2013. http://www.usatoday.com/story/sports/nfl/niners/2013/08/20/tarell-brown-bonehead-agent-two-million-dollar-escalator-lost/2678583/.

Bowles, Hannah Riley, and Kathleen L. McGinn. "Gender in Job Negotiations: A Two-Level Game." Harvard Business School, June 11, 2008. http://hbswk.hbs.edu/item/5935.html.

Bowman, Mark. "Braves Give Smoltz an Extension." MLB.com, April 26, 2007. http://mlb.mlb.com/news/article.jsp?ymd = 20070426&content_id = 1932258&vkey = news_mlb&fext = .jsp&c_id = mlb.

Bowman, Mark. "Francoeur, Braves Avoid Arbitration." MLB.com, February 19, 2009. http://atlanta.braves.mlb.com/news/article.jsp?ymd = 20090219&content_id = 3848322& vkey = news_atl&fext = .jsp&c_id = atl.

Caprino, Kathy. "5 Hidden Assumptions That Keep Women from Living Larger." *Forbes*, January 27, 2014. http://www.forbes.com/sites/kathycaprino/2014/01/27/5-hidden-assumptions-that-keep-women-from-living-larger.

Congress.gov. "S.84—Paycheck Fairness Act." Accessed February 24, 2014. http://beta.congress.gov/bill/113th/senate-bill/84.

Cox, Wendell. "Toward a Self Employed Nation?" *New Geography,* June 6, 2013. http://www.newgeography.com/content/003761-toward-a-self-employed-nation.

Farrar, Doug. "Elway's Last NFL Act Was All the Difference in Manning's Decision." Yahoo! Sports, March 21, 2012. http://sports.yahoo.com/blogs/nfl-shutdown-corner/elway-last-nfl-act-difference-manning-decision-043839848.html.

Gasink, John, and Jeff Weiss. "The 'Other' Party: Getting into the Mind of Your Negotiating Counterpart." *Ivey Business Journal,* July–August 2004. http://iveybusinessjournal.com/topics/the-workplace/the-other-party-getting-into-the-mind-of-your-negotiating-counterpart#.UwyvKIUwDeN.

Gladwell, Malcolm. *Blink: The Power of Thinking Without Thinking.* New York: Little, Brown, 2005.

Halvorson, Heidi Grant. "The Trouble with Bright Girls." *Psychology Today,* January 27, 2011. http://www.psychologytoday.com/blog/the-science-success/201101/the-trouble-bright-girls.

Harvard Law School. "Men, Women, and Status in Negotiations." March 21, 2013.

Lagace, Martha. "Negotiating Challenges for Women Leaders." Harvard Business School. October 3, 2003. http://hbswk.hbs.edu/item/3711.html.

Marder, Jenny. "Nyad's Feet Touch Sand, Swimmer Completes Historic 110-Mile Swim." PBS, September 2, 2013. http://www.pbs.org/newshour/rundown/nyad-closer-than-ever-to-completing-historic-cuba-to-florida-swim/.

Mayo Clinic. "Positive Thinking: Reduce Stress by Eliminating Negative Self-Talk." Accessed February 24, 2014. http://www .mayoclinic.org/positive-thinking/art-20043950.

Medvec, Victoria H., and Adam D. Galinsky. "Putting More on the Table: How Making Multiple Offers Can Increase the Final Value of the Deal." *Harvard Business Review,* April 1, 2005. http://hbr.org/product/putting-more-on-the-table-how-making-multiple-offe/an/N0504BPDF-ENG.

Medvec, Victoria H., Scott F. Madey, and Thomas Gilovich. "When Less Is More: Counterfactual Thinking and Satisfaction Among Olympic Medalists." *Journal of Personality and Social Psychology,* vol. 69, pp. 603–610, 1995.

"Moehler, Astros Exercise Option." ESPN.com, October 8, 2009. http://sports.espn.go.com/mlb/news/story?id = 4544158& campaign = rss&source = MLBHeadlines.

Nielsen. "U.S. Women Control the Purse Strings." Accessed February 24, 2014. http://www.nielsen.com/us/en/ newswire/2013/u-s--women-control-the-purse-strings.html.

Pynchon, Victoria. "Why Women Don't Negotiate (and What We Can Do About It)." *Forbes,* February 26, 2012. http://www.forbes .com/sites/dailymuse/2012/02/26/why-women-dont-negotiate-and-what-we-can-do-about-it/.

Salary.com. "Most People Don't Negotiate Due to Fear & Lack of Skills." Accessed February 24, 2014. www.salary.com/most-people-don-t-negotiate-due-to-fear-lack-of-skills/.

Thompson, Leigh. *Mind and Heart of the Negotiator.* 5th ed. Upper Saddle River, NJ: Prentice Hall, 2011.

Van Boven, Leaf, Thomas Gilovich, and Victoria Husted Medvec. "The Illusion of Transparency in Negotiations." *Negotiation Journal*, vol. 19, pp. 117–131, 2003.

Wertheim, L. Jon. "The Case for . . . Challenging the System." *Sports Illustrated,* September 9, 2013. http://sportsillustrated.cnn.com/vault/article/magazine/MAG1208607/index.htm.

WNBA. "WNBA Announces New Ownership for Atlanta Dream." Accessed February 26, 2014. http://www.wnba.com/news/dream_ownership_091029.html.

Women Don't Ask. "Women Don't Ask: Negotiation and the Gender Divide." Accessed February 24, 2014. http://www.womendontask.com/stats.html.

"Why Women Must Ask (The Right Way): Negotiation Advice from Stanford's Margaret A. Neale." *Forbes,* June 17, 2013. http://www.forbes.com/sites/dailymuse/2013/06/17/why-women-must-ask-the-right-way-negotiation-advice-from-stanfords-margaret-aneale/.

Index

About the Author

A top sports agent with two decades of experience, **Molly Fletcher** represented some of the biggest names in sports, including Doc Rivers, Billy Donovan, Tom Izzo, John Smoltz, Matt Kuchar, and Ernie Johnson, Jr.

Molly is now a professional speaker and runs her own consulting firm in Atlanta, Georgia. A popular corporate speaker, her clients include many Fortune 500 companies. She speaks to audiences around the country on topics related to business development, negotiation, leadership, and team building.

Molly is the author of two other books, *The 5 Best Tools to Find Your Dream Career* and *The Business of Being the Best*. She has been featured in numerous media outlets, including CNN, ESPN, *Sports Illustrated, USA Today,* and the *Wall Street Journal*.

A graduate of Michigan State University, Molly was a captain of the Spartans women's tennis team. She currently resides in Atlanta with her husband, Fred, and their three daughters.

Visit Molly's website: www.mollyfletcher.com